thank you for joining us!

Teresa :)

503-665--1505

Achieve Your Dreams
A Journey to Your Financial Freedom

By Teresa Noe

With help from Contributing Authors

ISBN 978-0-578-01002-1

Special Edition December 2008

Teresa Noe is a registered representative of and offers Securities
through NEXT Financial Group, Inc.

Member FINRA and SIPC

4WARD Financial Marketing, Inc is a wholly owned subsidiary of

NEXT Financial Holdings, Inc

Book is published by:

4WARD Financial Marketing, Inc.

FOREWORD

This book is the resulting collaboration of many associate professionals who share my vision to deliver the best guidance possible in an ongoing effort to help my clients achieve their dreams and goals.

I offer this book to show my appreciation for becoming and remaining Your Trusted Financial Team for Life.

TABLE OF CONTENTS

CHAPTER 1
Blending Your Tax and Investment Needs 1
Contributing Author Teresa Noe

CHAPTER 2
Building the "Long Walk" Relationship with Your Advisor 5
Contributing Author Lynn Berry

CHAPTER 3
Entrepreneurism 13
Contributing Author David Parker

CHAPTER 4
Back to the Fundamentals 37
 Contributing Author Thierry Sommers

CHAPTER 5
Planning for Income Tax Efficiency.. 49
Contributing Author John Lau, CFP®, CPA, M.S. (Taxation)

CHAPTER 6
Investing for Growth and Income with Stocks and Bonds.................... 59
Contributing Author C.J. Liepman

CHAPTER 7
Ten Exit Strategies for Highly Appreciated Real Estate 75
Contributing Author Larry Weiss, CPA, CSA

CHAPTER 8
College Savings 101 99
Contributing Author Jennifer Blake Karaczun

CHAPTER 9
Women, Wealth, and Worth 117
Contributing Author Julie Gneiser

CHAPTER 10
Qualified Plans for Business Owners.. 135
Contributing Author David Parker

CHAPTER 11
Planning Your Retirement 157
Contributing Author Anthony Untersee CFP

CHAPTER 12
Planning for Healthcare in Retirement....................................... 161
Contributing Author Richard Horner

CHAPTER 13
Business Succession Planning.. 191
Contributing Author Thomas C. Schmidt, Sr.

CHAPTER 14
The Seven Habits of Highly Successful Seniors...................................... 207
Contributing Author Charles J. Barley

CHAPTER 15
Making Your Retirement Money Last.. 225
Contributing Author Jim Spires

CHAPTER 16
The Missing Estate Plan.. 231
Contributing Author John Lau, CFP®, CPA, M.S. (Taxation)

Chapter 1

Blending Your Tax and Investment Needs

Contributing Author Teresa Noe

Have you ever been overwhelmed by the Tax Code and how it will affect you? Ever made financial decisions only to discover that you created an ugly tax situation? Ever tried to capitalize on a tax benefit only to learn that your investment decision lost you more money than it saved you in taxes?

You're not alone. These concepts plague thousands of your fellow investors. The simple solution is to find a professional who is well versed in both tax law and investment products. This is not easy, but it is certainly not impossible.

After all, there are tax implications in most investment decisions and investment implications in most tax decisions. A bad choice may affect your portfolio with reduced returns or make the Internal Revenue Service very happy with a larger year-end tax liability. You want to keep more of your hard-earned money, but not by hindering your portfolio or elating Uncle Sam with your tax payment!

To begin the process of finding a professional who can fill this need, you might first ask your current investment and/or tax professional. Ask about his or her background, and determine if you are already working with a professional who is well versed in both industries.

If so ... great! You may be done. If not, interview your professional by asking these questions:

- Who are the members of your associate network of professionals and how often do you meet with them?

- Do you have a no-charge avenue to information outside your expertise?

- Do you frequently use and nurture the relationship?

- What continuing education do you receive and what ongoing education does your network of professionals maintain?

Alternatively, if you currently use the services of a tax professional, but use a different financial planner and believe they are both doing a great job, then you can be much more proactive in coordinating their efforts. Here's a list of things to consider that will contribute to your overall financial health:

- After having your tax return completed each year, ask your tax preparer to provide a copy of the tax return to your financial planner. By the way, if you are doing your own tax return... stop! The Tax Code is far too complex, and missing available tax benefits could mean giving your money to Uncle Sam! If your financial planner is effective, he or she has been asking you for copies of your tax returns every year!

- Visit with your tax professional at least one time during each year, preferably during the last quarter. Bring your portfolio summary and ask him or her to review it for tax-planning opportunities. Should you sell anything to capture losses that can be used to offset gains? Should you commit additional money to your accounts? Should you convert your traditional individual retirement account (IRA) to a Roth IRA or set up and fund a different type of retirement account? Many of these issues may not affect your overall portfolio, but they are critical to resolve prior to year-end. If you wait until your tax preparation season, it may be too late to make needed changes.

- Visit with your financial planner at least once shortly after he or she has reviewed your tax return. Find out if you are positioned well given your tax bracket. Should you be using tax-preferred or tax-free products? If not, is your rate of return strong enough to outweigh the taxes being generated?

- Go one step further… facilitate a meeting with all your advisers so they can get to know each other and get a good picture of what you expect and why you believe it is important that they are all working under the same assumptions.

Now, this type of coordination can be a bit time-consuming, but it is certainly critical to your financial wealth. How does your right hand know what your left hand is doing, if not for the signals you send?

Finding one professional who can provide both tax and financial advice can eliminate your coordinating challenges. But understand that both industries are heavily regulated and there is a huge amount of information to know, so it is naturally a bit challenging for one person to know it all. However, as long as the professional is appropriately licensed in both arenas, he or she will have contacts who can provide expertise beyond that of your professional

Working with a professional who provides both tax and investment management services can not only save you money, but also (and maybe more importantly) save you hours of frustration. This unique full-service philosophy is available in all parts of the country, and it can be applied even further to mortgage and accounting services as well.

Start by consulting your existing professionals. If you have concerns, then either seek referrals from an adviser you trust or from reliable friends and associates who are already operating under this unique approach. Keep interviewing advisers until you find the one who will put your interests first, and who understands your desire to be well represented in all aspects of your financial health.

Chapter 2

Building the "Long Walk" Relationship with Your Advisor

Contributing Author Lynn Berry

It is only with the heart that one sees rightly; what is essential is invisible to the eye.

~Antoine De Saint-Exupery

Each of us lives our lives through a series of conversations. Conversations with family, friends, co-workers, and indeed everyone around us, help shape who we are, what we do, and even how we feel. The problem is that the conversations clients are having with their advisors are not deep enough, not meaningful enough, and in grave need of improvement.

As technologies continue to develop at an ever increasing pace, we seem to have lost a good deal of personal relationship development. We are no longer talking in the workplace; we don't talk at home, at school, in our neighborhoods, or communities. We have built ever smaller computers that hold an unfathomable mountain of information, yet we communicate less and less, making our relationships shallow. We have more money, and a better than 50 percent divorce rate. We have fancier houses and more broken homes than ever before. We've learned to make a living but not really make a life. Most of us do not even know our neighbors. Your advisor should, and could, have a profound impact on your life if you find the right one. Like an inspirational teacher or preacher or doctor who saved your life, you can find an advisor who can have the same impact. It is time to build a true "long walk relationship" with a trusted advisor who really listens and really cares. Your advisor must be willing to have deep and meaningful conversations with you today, tomorrow, and always.

Analyzing everyday conversations, and their effects on relationships, doesn't appear at first glace to be what a financial advisor should do best, but it should be. It is critical that your advisor really knows who you are, what you do, and more importantly, what are you trying to accomplish. That conversation cannot happen when the stopwatch is ticking at every meeting. Think about the conversations you have had of late with your advisors. Was the stopwatch ticking? Did you feel rushed, or were you made to feel quite at home?

Your relationship with your advisors should be long walk relationships. You cannot have a deep and meaningful relationship if you are only talking with your advisor, on the clock, about how much money you have, the current rates of return, the hot stock, or best mutual fund or variable product. It's not that those things are not important, they are, but it is not about the products, it's about you. It's not about your advisor, or her firm or his sales quota, it's about you. The only thing that matters is what's best for you, your family, or your business.

How can you begin to build a long walk relationship with your financial advisor? First and foremost, you must begin with asking questions. You need to know your advisor as much as he or she needs to know you. A good advisor will be your liaison or personal financial coach leading your financial team to success. A good advisor will interface between you and your attorney and you and your certified public accountant (CPA) or personal money manager. A good advisor will stand in your corner. He or she will lead your team, so it is important to find a caring and knowledgeable team player as your advisor. Not all advisors are created equal. Putting in a bit of effort to ask good questions can save you from the harsh discovery that you've given your assets to a simple salesperson, and not a trusted advisor who is putting your interests first.

The trusted advisor typically works in a client-centric organization built around the attitudes of confidence, caring, and integrity. A client-centric organization is one that revolves around client needs, not corporate needs. The backbone of that organization is caring. It is quite difficult to fake caring; you can feel real caring when you are in its presence. You will know, too, by the questions your advisor is asking. Are the advisors asking you values questions, goal questions, and life questions, or are they only asking you how much money you have? If you are looking for the long walk relationship, it will be as important to pay attention to the questions you are being asked as it will be to formulate good questions of your own to ask the advisor. Let's take a look at some good questions to ask an advisor before you agree to a meeting.

You may have met your potential advisor through a marketing campaign, like a seminar are expo event. Make sure you pick up a card so you can call to set up a simple phone meeting. You may have been referred to him or her from a friend or family member too, but the process will be the same. First, you may want to check your potential advisor's credentials. It is easier than you may think.

The Financial Industry Regulatory Authority (FINRA) is the largest nongovernmental regulator for all securities firms doing business with the United States public. All told, FINRA oversees nearly 5,100 brokerage firms, about 173,000 branch offices, and more than 669,000 registered securities representatives. You can simply visit FINRA on its web at www.finra.org. Once you are there, go to the investor information tab, scroll down to the section called "Check your

Broker." You can then print a PDF report detailing your advisor's licensing, current registration, past employment, and whether he or she has any customer complaints or regulatory issues. There is no sense in working with someone you cannot trust.

In your quest for this long walk relationship advisor, do not be too distracted by tenure and designations. While it may be comforting to know you are working with a Certified Financial Planner, it does not mean he or she is really a better advisor. Also, the number of years one has been "in the business" is no guarantee of competence. It may be very beneficial if the advisor has been committed to lifetime growth; however, a few advisors have one year of experience that they have simply repeated 25 times.

Once you are comfortable with the conversation, you need to find out what the advisor must know from you, to determine if you are a fit for his or her services. Typically, the best advisors specialize in helping a particular type of individual or group. That could be pre-retirees of a certain age or baby boomers ages 45 to 65. They may have net worth minimums or investable asset minimums. A good advisor will answer that question without any hesitation.

Finally, you will want to ask if the advisor has an identifiable process that you will follow should you choose to work with the firm. Again, the best advisors will be able to easily communicate their process to you. If you feel your questions have been answered to your satisfaction, it would be a good idea to set a time to meet in person to learn more about the process. The advisor will likely have a list of financial documents you should bring to this meeting to discover and decide if this will be the long walk relationship you both are looking for. This process is often called the wealth strategy process.

The Wealth Strategy Process

1. **Introductory Meeting or Seminar Workshop**
2. **Personal Meeting to Discover and Decide**
3. **Planning Presentation and Solutions Meeting**
4. **Implementation Meeting**
5. **Quarterly Progress Meeting**

Your Wealth Strategy

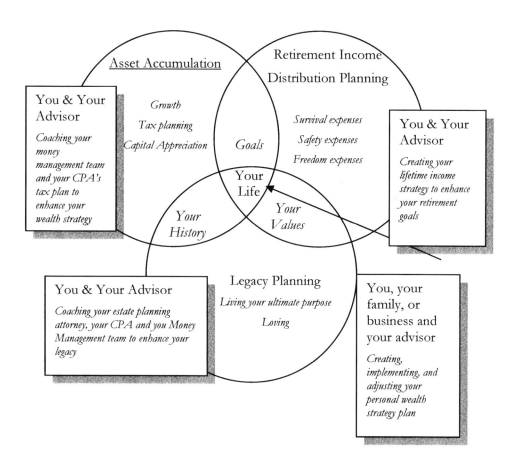

In your first personal meeting, you will get to know your advisor on a personal level by the questions he or she asks you. This is the meeting of discovery for both of you, but the advisor will be interviewing you. By the time you have spent about an hour together, you will know if you are in the presence of a professional and you will feel if he or she really cares about you. It will be clear to you whether you have found your trusted advisor or simply a salesperson. If you have spent the hour with a salesperson, you will feel spent when you are done. If you have spent the time with a trusted advisor, you will feel inspired and energized to take the next step toward true financial success, as defined by you and your needs.

So what kind of questions can you expect from truly good advisors?

First stop, you'll talk about your history. How can they help you get where you want to go if they have no idea where you have been? Your history helped shape your fears, your hopes, your values, and, frankly, your entire life. Your advisor should spend some time to really get to know you, not just your pocketbook. The real goal for building a solid relationship with your advisor is to make sure your future is better than your past. Example questions might be, "Tell me about your life's work," or "Tell me about the best (worst) financial decision you ever made," or perhaps, "If you could pass one financial lesson on to your children or grandchildren, what would that be?"

Second stop in the interview will likely be your goals and your values. In order for your advisor to build a long walk relationship with you, he or she will require a deep understanding of what is important to you. How do you define balance in you life? What is the most important thing about money to you? How do you define success at home, at work, and with your money?

Next it is important for your advisor to find out where you are headed. That leads to a very important question from a company called the Strategic Coach and its founder Dan Sullivan, "Three years from today, if we are having this conversation, what needs to have happened between now and then, for you to feel you have made progress and our relationship has been beneficial to you, your family, or your business?" This will help you and your advisor determine your survival needs, your safety needs, and you freedom goals. You must paint a picture, you and your advisor, of what you are shooting for from the understanding of your past, your values, and your dreams. Once that is clearly articulated, then and only then should the conversation turn to your assets.

Once your advisor has a good understanding of who you are, where you want to be, and from where you are starting, a comprehensive wealth strategy can be developed on your behalf. That strategy will center on the solutions necessary to bring you closer to financial success. Your advisor will share the solutions and likely need to be introduced to your CPA if you have one. While your advisor may be a certified public account, it is very likely he or she won't be. Your advisor will always be willing to work in tandem with your accounting professional to make sure you are reaching your goals. Your advisor will not likely be an attorney, but will have knowledge of the ramifications of not having a will or a trust in your plan. A professional advisor will have no trouble facilitating all the partnerships you need for success.

Creating the plan and coaching the relationships you need to reach your goal are just the beginning when you have selected the right advisor. Remember, this is a long walk relationship. That means a partnership of sorts. This plan is not the commandments written in stone, but more like a potter's wheel where the plan evolves and changes as you evolve grow and change. Together, you and your advisor should be talking, having meaningful conversations, and taking your initial handshake to a great big hug. You will create a long walk through asset growth and accumulation, through income distribution and pure financial freedom, to the sunset of your legacy. Your advisor should be with you, to share, to be there, to understand, and to see you, your family, and your business from the perspective of your goals. The process does not have to be complicated. Life is complicated enough. With good, solid, deep conversations, you with your advisor as your coach can compile the team you need to make your dreams come true. As information comes pouring in at a faster and faster clip, let your advisor be your "human browser," navigating the thousands of mutual funds, endless stock picks, oil and gas programs, real estate investment trusts, variable life, variable annuities, and an endless supply of the "new and the improved," because it is really far less about the products. It is all about you.

Chapter 3

Entrepreneurism

Contributing Author David Parker

I s entrepreneurship right for you? Ultimately, only you can answer that question. However, careful consideration of several points may help you in coming up with the right answer.

Entrepreneurship can be very rewarding. Some may become very wealthy. Others may relish the opportunity to be in charge, to make their own decisions as to the direction of their company. On the other hand, the risks are many. Entrepreneurs lack the access to the abundant resources and sophisticated support systems that large organizations provide. Many start-ups fail within the first year. Being responsible for the success or failure of the company is often very stressful for the entrepreneur and his or her family.

A High Need for Achievement

Although studies of entrepreneurs reveal considerable diversity in terms of external factors such as industry, location, and amount of capital, there does appear to be some similarity of internal factors—personality traits—that are shared by many successful entrepreneurs. Harvard's David McClelland has found that many of the successful entrepreneurs he has studied possess a high need for achievement. He found that there are five common characteristics possessed by people with this need.

First, a person who has a high need for achievement likes situations enabling him or her to take personal responsibility and get personal credit for results. He does not like to wait for others to resolve problems; instead, he likes to take it upon himself to make decisions and get things done. Obviously, we are not talking about the typical team player here, but rather one who enjoys individual responsibility and is turned on by personal achievement.

A second characteristic is preference for intermediate levels of risk. This is not the "high-rolling risk takers" that entrepreneurs are often thought to be, nor is it an overwhelming need for security. Successful entrepreneurs invariably wanted enough risk "to make it interesting" but avoided risk levels that posed major threats to success. Undoubtedly, taking some risk is part of the fun, but achieving the goal is the primary motivator.

Preference for unambiguous and timely feedback is a third characteristic. A person with this characteristic always wants to know what is going on, what areas of the business are successful, and what areas need to be improved. What percentage have sales improved this month? How much greater is the cost for advertising than we predicted? If there are any problems, this information needs to be known, so that the problems can be solved as rapidly as possible. The department head that wants results now, not at the end of next quarter, demonstrates this need.

Fourth is the preference for situations permitting innovative and novel solutions. Often, entrepreneurs are faced with unexpected problems, requiring new methods to solve those problems. A person with this need enjoys the challenge of these situations. Constant attempts to come up with new approaches to creative financing, for example, might reflect such a need.

Finally, a strong future orientation is a frequent characteristic. Entrepreneurs see possibilities for the future, and focus on that rather than the problems. They take time to plan ahead to take advantage of future opportunities. Financial analysts who prefer estimating the probabilities of future scenarios as opposed to compiling historical data reflect a need for this type of situation.

Perhaps the most interesting aspect of this theory is the role that money plays in entrepreneurial motivation. Money does not, in and of itself, directly motivate the successful entrepreneur. Rather, it acts as a scorecard, a feedback source, for the extent of achievement that has been attained. Entrepreneurial researchers Jeffrey Timmons, Leonard Smollen, and Alexander Dingee cite the example of an entrepreneur who successfully built up his business and sold it for several million dollars.

At age 40, this recent millionaire announced that he was leaving New York City to move to Florida. He and his wife were going to buy a fancy condominium and large yacht, and live the good life. Within two weeks the man phoned his former venture capitalist and told him he was bored stiff, could not stand the peace and quiet, and was "coming back to build another company." He needed to achieve.

Money is obviously important to the entrepreneur, both as a means and as an end, but most researchers agree that the need for achievement takes precedence over monetary reward in motivating successful entrepreneurs.

The profile of a successful entrepreneur frequently embodies traits that are neither necessary nor sufficient in all circumstances—too many other variables exist that influence success. Such a profile can, however, provide one with some insight as to whether he or she possesses some of the personality traits found among many successful entrepreneurs.

What Causes a Business to Fail?

We have seen how having a high need to achieve and an appreciation for the use of money is characteristic of successful entrepreneurs. This alone does not make a new business successful. In fact, the statistics regarding the failure rate of new businesses can be downright depressing. Despite conflicting estimates of failure rates, it appears that roughly 10 percent of all start-ups fail within 12 months, and after three years, one out of every three businesses has failed. By no means is an entrepreneur's success assured.

Naturally, the question that comes to mind is: What causes a business to fail? The answer, it seems, is poor management. Data compiled by the United States Small Business Administration suggest that almost all business failures stem from owner or manager error. Dunn & Bradstreet has found that 91.9 percent of all business failure is caused, at least in part, by inexperience or incompetence. It also found that 52.3 percent of business failure is due to inadequate sales experience, and 28.9 percent of business failure is due to heavy operating expenses.

Interestingly enough, basic causes of business failure were well known over a century ago. The following quotation, taken from the February 1903 edition of "World of Work," attests to mismanagement's timelessness as a cause of failure:

> There can be no exact science of success; but the hint that this table of wrecks gives is that a man of character and good judgment, who by his native endowment will avoid the perils that beset incompetence, needs to make very sure of enough capital, and then that competition need not frighten him.

Behavioral scientists have long been intrigued with man's tendency to attribute successes to personal endeavor and failures to external factors. The entrepreneur is no exception. The failing entrepreneur frequently attributes the inadequate sales problem to "just not enough business out there" when, in truth, it is probably attributed to inadequate market research or poorly planned sales tactics. Similarly, unreasonable overhead charges are frequently blamed for heavy operating expenses as opposed to unreasonable estimates during the planning stage.

Taken collectively, the literature on business failure suggests that poor management is the primary culprit, and poor planning is the hallmark of poor management.

The absence of effective planning is a major cause of incalculable financial losses as well as the social and psychological trauma that frequently accompanies business failures.

Given the prevalence of poor planning among business start-ups, the entrepreneur who plans effectively is well poised to meet the competition. What, then, constitutes effective planning for new ventures?

The New Business Plan

A formal business plan is a comprehensive document describing a proposed new business or a new venture for an existing business. Usually requiring several months and anywhere from a few hundred to several thousand dollars for preparation, the new business plan describes in detail what the venture is all about and provides sufficient evidence of potential. Sometimes referred to as a feasibility study, the business plan not only tells us why the deal will work, but actually plays an important role in helping to make it work.

The new business plan serves at least four purposes:

- Forces the entrepreneur to organize thoughts logically

There seems to be some magic in using the legal pad and felt-tip pen to push from the head-scratching stage to a well-conceived idea. Organizing thoughts on paper, or on a computer screen, will usually reveal whether the deal makes sense. In essence, developing the plan provides the self-discipline needed for exploring the proposed venture from all angles.

- Provides information for investment or credit decisions

The business plan enables the venture capitalist, lender, or private investor with vital information to make informed decisions. Rest assured that the new business plan is not simply a good idea. It is an essential step in raising capital. The businessperson without a plan will be immediately conspicuous and will be turned away by a venture capitalist.

- Convinces a reviewer you have done your homework

The initial concept may sound good, but how thorough is the preparation? Does the plan describe a good marketing idea, or does it specify a comprehensive marketing plan including, for example, new client potential, advertising, public relations, and pricing policies? Simply put, the business plan shows not only what the entrepreneur thinks, but also how he or she thinks. Attention to detail in the plan is usually indicative of attention to detail in the business.

- Provides a blueprint for building the business

Once the financing has been arranged, the plan becomes a reference manual outlining who will do what, when, and how.

Invariably, the manual must be modified, updated, or even rewritten, but its content can serve as a valuable basis for making important decisions.

Before starting to put together the plan, you should prepare a detailed outline listing all the topics to be covered. This will help you determine the information necessary to develop the business
plan and organize it into clearly defined sections. Business plans usually have separate sections discussing the management team, the product/service, marketing and sales plans, and financial information. A brief synopsis of each of these topics follows.

Your Mission Statement

The first section of the business plan revolves around the mission statement, a sentence or two explaining the company's reason for existing. The more specific the initial definition, the better the owner understands the market niche the firm is trying to carve.

"Happy Computers is a microcomputer reseller in Los Angeles, California," is not nearly as refined a starting point as, "Happy Computers, a value-added reseller in Los Angeles, is in business to serve the office and field equipment needs of Southern California construction companies with 20 employees or less."

Developing such business descriptions seems simple enough, but according to Carol Anderson, a Norwood, Massachusetts-based consultant who helps microcomputer resellers tackle management needs, many resellers never get past this initial planning hurdle.

"When you're in a small business environment with less than 50 employees, it's easy to get caught up in the day-to-day operation and never look up," she says. "Many resellers have a plan in their head, but they're not sure how to implement it. Since the employees don't have a clear-cut mission, there's no specific direction for everyone to move in."

A few years ago, Anderson produced a 30-page booklet for the National Office Products Association (NOPA) to help members get the planning ball rolling. Appropriately titled "Blueprint for Business Planning: Marketing and Financial Strategies for Computer Resellers," the booklet defines the process of crystallizing a mission statement and proceeds onward with the details of a business plan. "A good business plan has a life of its own which changes and evolves with the business," writes Anderson in the introduction of the booklet. "It is a compass, setting the course and steering the company."

The Management Team

This section of the business plan is one of the most important. Before agreeing to finance a company, a professional investor will conduct a thorough reference check on each member of the management team and how the team member's skills or background will contribute to the company's success. This should also be supported by a detailed resume included in the appendix.

Here, you should describe the planned organizational structure, including officers, directors, board members, and consultants, if any. If the team lacks any critical skills, indicate how and when you will recruit people possessing these skills. Include a brief description of any incentive plans, such as stock options or profit sharing plans.

How will you recruit and train personnel? This can be critical if you must deliver good service to your customers.

The Product/Service

The description of the product/service should not be too detailed. However, be prepared to answer many questions about the research, development, and manufacturing of the product/service and, with your permission, to send this information to a consultant for evaluation. If you have already built a working model or prototype of the product, you should include a photograph of it. If not, it would be helpful to include an artist's rendering.

The business plan should also explain how you will manufacture the product or perform the service. If research and development (R&D) is required, you should identify key development goals and list the time requirements and approximate costs for meeting them. Any inherent technical risks as well as other technologies that will affect the product or service should also be explained. It is helpful to mention whether the product/service is or can be patented or otherwise protected by trademarks, copyrights, or trade secret protection programs.

Researching the Market

Once a firm has clarified specifically why it is in business, the next stage is to identify the market. What is the demographic makeup of the territory? Is it dominated by small, medium-sized, or Fortune 500 companies?

If a firm has been operating up until now without doing such research, the leaders might be surprised by what they learn in the planning process. A variety of references can be called upon to help in market research: local chambers of commerce, the Small Business Administration, trade associations, even the public library. Make value judgments about the data, however, for often statistics alone can be misleading.

If you are looking at very large opportunities, it is easy to get statistics to justify expectations. Business consultants know that new and old firms can easily become mired in terms of personnel and resources without any great payoff. They fail to understand the market well enough to deliver a measurable result.

Thoroughly research competitors. What are their strengths and weaknesses? Do not be surprised to find some formidable opponents.

Marketing and Sales Plans

This section of the business plan must convince prospective investors that there is a market for the product/service. Include a description of the market, an explanation of what drives the market (why customers will buy), how it is segmented and distributed, market size (in dollar volume and number of customers), and how you expect to achieve a level of market penetration.

In addition, include a list of major competitors and assess their respective strengths and weaknesses. If the product will compete directly with another company's products/services, compare their performance and price.

Generally, the price charged should be determined by how much the market will pay for the product, not the cost to manufacture and sell it. If the maximum selling price will not enable you to sell the product or service at a profit, it may be necessary to modify the product/service.

Every successful competitor will have identified an edge, and you should do the same. How will you differentiate yourself? What are your marketing plans? Short-term vertical opportunities may be hot for only a month or two, so it is imperative to move quickly. The business plan notes this. For more long-term markets, the plan details how to develop solid leads.

Financial Statements

The most critical chapter in a thorough business plan cuts right to the bottom line. Every aspect of the operation's financials—budgets, balance sheets, profit-and-loss statements—will be spelled out. Projections should also be made and the operation's financial health should be reviewed regularly.

These figures should be used not only as a guideline but also to measure actual performance. Too many owners do not get directly involved in accounting. Instead, they turn the responsibility over to a bookkeeper. The business owners then do not have a real understanding of profit margins and inventory management.

One thing that usually stands out in companies that fail is an inventory problem. Either the business is not buying properly or it is not selling at the right margins. Both areas can be monitored with the business plan.

Try to look at the month as it stacks up against the business plan, after discounting unusual big orders or bonuses. For instance, at the beginning of a year, one firm had not invested heavily in its service department but the amount of money it was making was higher than projected. It was time to take another look at service and adjust the business plan. It invested capital, adjusted its rates to match those of competitors, and never missed a beat—but profits increased.

Funding Request

The funding request section of the business plan should state how much money is needed, why it is needed, and what will be done with it. The explanation of what will be done with the funds should be consistent with financial projections. If you are seeking seed capital, sales, income, and cash flow projections as well as information on manufacturing, selling, and administrative costs should be included.

If, however, you are seeking a subsequent round of financing, five-year cash flow, profit-and-loss, and balance sheet projections will be required, as well as current audited financial statements. By having the statements audited by an independent accounting firm, potential investors may be more inclined to place reliance on the figures.

The Executive Summary

Because investors may not be willing to search through an entire business plan to locate its essential elements, the highlights of the plan should be presented in the "executive summary." A well-written summary should occupy no more than one or two pages and enable a prospective investor to quickly determine whether the plan deserves further study.

It also can serve another important use if you are planning to send the business plan to investors with whom you are not acquainted. You may want to send just the summary with a cover letter. This will protect the confidential details of the plan and can save printing and postage costs.

Legal Entities for Business

One of the most important decisions you will have to make is under which type of legal entity you will operate. This decision affects everything in your business, including the ease of formation, organizational structure, the amount of legal liability, the amount of taxes you will have to pay, and even the ability to change ownership or dissolve the business. There are four basic forms to consider: sole proprietor, partnership, C-corporation, and S-corporation. Each has its own set of advantages and disadvantages.

Sole Proprietorship

A sole proprietorship is the easiest and least expensive type of business to start. As the title indicates, the owner is a single proprietor with total ownership of all assets and responsibility for all liabilities.

To start your business under this form, you may simply need to buy a license (or a retail vendor license) for doing business in your city or county.

If you are operating your business under a name other than your name (fictitious name, dba = doing business as), you will need to register it with the secretary of state. After you have done a name search and after you have registered this name with the secretary of state, it must be published in a newspaper or periodical authorized by the office of the secretary of state. Now you can open a bank account under your company name.

Advantages of Sole Proprietorship

- It is the easiest and least expensive form of business to start.

- The owner receives 100 percent of the profit or 100 percent of losses that offset other earned income.

- It requires the minimum processing of legal documentation.

- The sole proprietor maintains complete ownership and control of the operation.

- The sole proprietor is the ultimate decision maker and has the flexibility to make decisions quickly to take advantage of a market opportunity.

- Tax filing for the sole proprietor is simple. There is no double taxation. All income and expenses from the business are reported through the owner on Schedule C of the 1040 tax form

Disadvantages of Sole Proprietorship

- The sole proprietor, while maintaining complete ownership and control of the operation, has complete responsibility for the liabilities of the firm. The sole proprietor has no protection from personal liability for all debts. Everything he or she owns, both business and personal assets, can be used as payment for business debts.

- As the sole decision maker, the sole proprietor has the burden of being accountable. You may not have a management team to share the responsibilities of day-to-day tasks and decisions, successes, and failures. It is strongly recommended that you have at your disposal an independent board of advisors and consultants to give you guidance and symbolically hold you accountable for good solid decisions.

- If the owner dies, there may be legal complications.

- The possibility of the owner's death may cause suppliers to terminate their relationship and cause creditors to call their loans.

- When the owner dies, the business is terminated.

- The sole proprietor is limited in fund-raising capacity equal to his or her net worth.

- The sole proprietor cannot transfer the business to a partner or to others.

- Sole proprietors are not employees; therefore, they cannot deduct certain expenses that a corporation may deduct.

- The sole proprietor is limited to his or her skills, capabilities, and talents unless subcontractors or employees are used.

Partnership

A partnership is a group of two or more people sharing ownership and responsibilities in a company. The partnership arrangement can be either formal or informal, written or a handshake. There are two types of partnerships—general and limited.

A general partner shares the liabilities as well as the assets of the firm, as does the sole proprietor. Each of the partner's personal assets can also be held as payment for debt of the partnership.

A limited partner makes an investment into the business, but cannot take an active management role in the day-to-day operations. Unlike the general partner, the limited partner's liabilities are only attached to the amount of money invested and not to personal assets. If you are a limited partner, you must be careful not to change your status to an active management role. If your limited partner status changes, so does your limited liability. You would then be subject to debts being settled against your personal assets.

As in any relationship or marriage, there are many human relation variables that need to be addressed to determine the compatibility of the partnership. This can be very difficult. Just as in any marriage, there may be ups and downs in a business relationship. If you choose to form a partnership for your business, you must be very careful with whom you join hands and wallets. You must also be careful to establish the proper legal contracts to protect all parties and to state very clearly what each partner's role is and how it is to be carried out.

Rights and Obligations of Partners

In their book, *Starting and Managing the Small Business*, Arthur Kuriloff and John Hemphill, Jr., have neatly outlined the Uniform Partnership Act as developed by the National Commissioners on Uniform State Laws.

The relationship of partners in the conduct of business has been spelled out in the Uniform Partnership Act. Many states have adopted the act in its entirety, while others have enacted variations of it. You should follow the legislation in force in your state if you enter into a partnership. In any event, the Uniform Partnership Act gives useful guidelines for a partnership by outlining both rights and obligations of partners.

RIGHTS: Under the Uniform Partnership Act, each partner has the right to:

- Share in the management and conduct of the business.
- Share in the profits of the firm.
- Receive repayment of contributions.
- Receive indemnification for, or return of, payments made on behalf of the partnership.
- Receive interest on additional advances made to the business.
- Have access to the books and records of the partnership.
- Have formal accounting of partnership affairs.

OBLIGATIONS: Under the act, each partner has the obligation to:

- Contribute toward losses sustained by the partnership.
- Work for the partnership without pay in the customary sense, but rather for a share of the profits.
- Submit to majority vote, or arbitration, when differences arise about the conduct of affairs of the business.
- Give other partners any information known personally about partnership affairs.
- Account to the partnership for all profits coming from any partnership transaction, or from partnership property.

Advantages of Partnerships

- Partnerships are fairly easy to form.
- The owners share the risk between themselves.
- There is access to diverse management skills and a larger pool of talent.
- There is no double taxation; income is taxed through each individual partner and not the partnership.
- Division of profits is based on the partnership agreement.
- There is access to a larger pool of capital than sole proprietorships can access.
- There is the ability to attract other partners.
- There is little governmental regulation.

Disadvantages of Partnerships

- In a general partnership, each partner is responsible for 100 percent of all debts, holding their personal as well as business assets liable, regardless of which partner made the commitment.

- In a limited partnership, the limited partner is liable for only the total investment made.

- As each partner shares in the liabilities, they also share in the profits.

- Upon the death of any partner, the partnership is dissolved.

- Dissolution of an existing partnership requires legal procedures.

- Either your or your partners' values may change over time, causing disunity and conflict in making decisions.

- Partners are bound by law of agency.

- There is limited capability for capital accumulation.

C-Corporation

A C-corporation is a legal entity. Its ownership is offered to the public. It is a separate entity formed by the state that pays taxes and is itself liable for all debts. It is, in essence, a third-party individual that in the eyes of the law is a living and breathing person and as such can accept the responsibility of assuming liabilities.

A corporation is more difficult to form than a sole proprietorship or partnership and can be formed only by complying with the state laws governing such formation and by fulfilling certain statutory requirements.

Although forming your company as a corporation puts the liability of debts in the hands of the corporation itself, this does not always hold true for small start-up companies. Many entrepreneurs find that to get financing, they must personally guarantee the loan before it can be approved. In this case, if the debts are not paid, the personal assets can be seized from the owner. Therefore, you can see that there may still be some limited liability as a C-corporation when starting your enterprise.

Advantages of C-Corporations

- The company continues to exist despite any ownership changes.
- You have an increased ability to raise capital as a result of the sale of stock.
- Each corporation must establish a board of directors that may provide valuable management assistance.
- You can have limited or no personal liability.
- Transfer of ownership is easier.
- There is a larger pool of skilled talent and knowledge.
- There is potential for economies of scales in operations.

Disadvantages of C-Corporations

- They are much more complicated and expensive to start up.
- There are many more legal requirements, reports, and tax returns. It is expensive to support the reporting requirements for C-corporations.

- You must adhere to government regulations regarding meetings of the board of directors (usually a meeting once every quarter is required). You must maintain board meeting minutes and document all major actions.

- Earnings are double taxed, once on the corporation and once on the personal salary or dividends you receive from the corporation.

- The potential for loss of control by the founders of the corporation exists.

Taxation

An ordinary corporation may elect to be taxed as an S-corporation, provided several criteria are met. For example, there cannot be more than 35 shareholders (a husband and a wife are counted as one shareholder); no shareholder may be a non-resident alien.

Under this election, corporate incomes flow through to the stockholder's income tax return.

The corporation does not pay income taxes; the stockholders record the income on their individual tax returns. The stockholders are taxed on the total corporate income, although not all of it may have been distributed. No double taxation is encountered under the S-corporation form. An S-corporation formed after 1983 must have the same tax year as its owners (generally, a calendar year).

Before electing this form of corporation for tax purposes, the electors should be thoroughly aware of all aspects of S-corporation requirements as well as the impact that such an election will have on after-tax cash flows. Such an election may or may not be an advantage, depending on the particular situation.

As with other legal forms of business, an attorney should be consulted prior to enterprise creation. This is especially true because some of the aspects of this law that might affect your business and your decision about type of legal entity may have changed.

Advantages of S-Corporations

- If the corporation expects to lose money in the early years of operation, and the shareholders will have income from other sources, the corporate losses will shelter the income from other sources.

- Because of the tax bracket the shareholders are in, there can be tax savings if the expected profits of the S-corporation are split among the shareholders.

- The business is such that the corporation does not need to retain a significant portion of its profits.

Disadvantages of S-Corporations

- You may have only up to 35 shareholders, limiting your level of financing.

- A non-resident alien may not take a part ownership in the corporation.

- No shareholder can be a partnership or corporation.

- The corporation can have only one class of common stock and no preferred stock.

- The tax laws regarding the S-corporation are very complex.

- When an S-corporation begins to produce very high levels of taxable income, it would be a good time to change to a C-corporation and begin collecting profits in the corporation. The Internal Revenue Service (IRS) will allow you to change to a C-corporation status.

The Selection Process

From the above legal entities, you should select the one that is most advantageous to you. Generally, with a new venture, the sole proprietorship is preferable, unless you need large financing for your project. The description of your business will take on the characteristics of the legal form you choose.

Additional Sources

A variety of sources can help you develop a business plan. A firm may receive assistance from a franchiser or strategic planning program sponsored by a major vendor. Personalized consultants may be enlisted, such as the Hamilton, New York-based American Management Association (AMA), which offers the Strategic Planning Process, an intensive program that analyzes every nook and cranny of planning for profit.

Such programs take a substantial financial investment—in the thousands for the AMA's one- to three-day seminars—but when finished, a detailed business plan will be in place.

The important thing in developing a business plan is that you do it and do it right. One approach is to retain a local financial planner trained in guiding small businesses in the development of a business plan.

If all this preparation seems a bit beyond your capacity for organizing, opportunities that are more appealing might be found in the area of franchising.

Franchise Opportunities

Franchising has put more people into business successfully than any other concept since capitalism. Approaching almost $400 billion in annual trade, franchising now constitutes almost half of U.S. retail sales. Unlike conventional business start-ups, franchises boast a remarkable success rate.

The most common type of franchise within the financial services industry is the trade name franchise. This arrangement enables, for example, the entrepreneur/independent financial planner to be identified with the franchiser's name and allows him or her to market a broad array of investment products and financial services for diverse clientele.

Franchises deserve the attention of prospective entrepreneurs/ independent financial planners. Advantages for the franchise include management and marketing counseling and training, strong due diligence, breadth and depth of investment products and services, financial support systems in the start-up phase, expeditious trading capabilities, and other services designed to enhance and ensure the initial and long-term success of the entrepreneur/independent financial planner.

Summary

In summary, many factors contribute to new business success, but certain personality characteristics appear frequently among successful entrepreneurs. Despite substantial failure rates, there is an easily identifiable cause in most cases—poor management.

Poor planning is usually at the root of poor management, and knowing how to prepare an effective new business plan can help the future entrepreneur fend off this ever-present problem. Although effective planning may increase chances for success, it is not always necessary in formulating the initial idea or basic concept.

America was built on entrepreneurship and continues to grow because of those enterprising individuals. May your business grow and prosper!

Sources:

United States Small Business Administration

Dun & Bradstreet report

Financial Planning Consultants, Inc.

Arthur H. Kuriloff, John M. Hemphill, Jr., Starting and Managing the Small Business (New York; McGraw-Hill, Inc., 1988).

Sherman A. Timmins, Ph.D., A Guide For Starting A New Small Business in the Toledo Metropolitan Area (Toledo: Small Business Institute, 1986).

Chapter 4

Back to the Fundamentals

Contributing Author Thierry Sommers

It is amazing what a child's soccer team can teach us. The basics of investing and sports are very similar. Everything begins by mastering the basics, practicing over and over the simple things until they become second nature. When soccer practice begins, the kids complain that they have to practice passing, dribbling, and running. They'd rather just start playing the game and avoid the pain and boredom of practice.

Most people's investment strategy can be compared to being the weekend warrior who spends a lot of time worried about money but very little time learning how money works and the strategies needed to build a successful financial plan. People frequently do nothing and hope things work out. They treat investments like a hobby and, when they lose interest, they lose their focus. These strategies really do not work; like learning a sport, you cannot play well unless you have some of the basic skills. The other strategies are like the weekend warriors who come to play with little or no preparation. They are surprised when they tear a muscle or they are sore the next day. The same could be said about people who dive into investments like stocks, bonds, real estate, commodities, and hedge funds. You need to learn both defense and how to protect yourself and your family from losses and offense so you know how to keep adding points and gaining wealth. This chapter breaks investing down to the basics, so you can see how all the pieces come together. Remember, you own the team (your investments) and, as the owner, it is important to have coaches in place to implement your personal goals.

There are many things you can do with your hard-earned money; the first is to keep cash, the second is to lend your cash out for interest, and the third is to own your investments, with the goal that they are to grow in wealth over time. They key word that is often overlooked is "time." Children develop skills over time, not overnight, and building your wealth takes time. You must first learn the foundation or core values. Once you understand the basics, sophisticated investment strategies become easier to understand.

The Five Basic Accounts

The basic positions, or pieces of the puzzle, are five accounts, sometimes called the CIA, catastrophic account, GIA, IRA, and SRA. Each account has a specific advantage and disadvantage. Remember that none of us is perfect and there are no perfect investments.

Cash Investment Account

A cash investment account (CIA) is otherwise known as emergency money. The CIA is really one of the hardest accounts to manage. People tend to consider credit cards as emergency money. In reality, credit cards are a great tool but are overused and tend to give us less control of our finances. CIA is considered to be cash, savings accounts, or money market funds. You should be able to have access to this investment within 24 hours. The general rule of thumb is to have three to six months of living expenses (six months if you are self-employed) in this account. This account is to be used only for an emergency. You should take a few moments to consider what an emergency would be for you. Typical emergencies include career changes, layoffs, medical time off, and home and car repairs. Some people treat the Holidays as an emergency and they turn to credit cards when they do not have enough money for Holiday gifts. Holidays happen every year, so there should be no surprises if you set up a separate account. When people have emergency accounts set up, then they can take their destiny into their own hands if the unforeseen occurs.

Every investment has advantages and disadvantages. One great part of having cash and low debt is that you have control. How often have you heard that "cash is king." The disadvantage of too much cash is that over a long period you may lose principal to inflation (the silent thief) and to taxes (the more visible thief). Here is an example of the effects of inflation and taxes on someone's emergency accounts:

$100,000.00 in savings account getting 4% interest with 3% inflation:

$100,000.00 will generate $4,000.00 of income at a tax rate of:

     10% = $400.00 in taxes

     15% = $600.00 in taxes

     20% = $800.00 in taxes

     25% = $1,000.00 in taxes

     28% = $1,120.00 in taxes

     30% = $1,200.00 in taxes

So, take the income and subtract your taxes and that will be your *real* income.

Inflation over a longer period averages around 3.2 percent; this includes food, housing, utilities, computers, credit cards, and services. Each item has a different inflation rate because some costs go down, often in manufactured products that tend to become less expensive (deflation). A prime example is the flat panel television, which is becoming more affordable. Another type of deflation is getting more for your money where computers are concerned. The prices stay about the same; however, the companies increase speed or memory space. Items that tend to be more inflationary are items that really affect retirees (e.g., the price of travel on a flight may be consistent, but there are fewer meals and snacks and the planes are more crowded). Other inflationary items for retirees include medical doctor visits, insurance, medicine, and home health; prices for all are rising faster than the inflation rate of 3 percent. Additional inflationary items include food, personal services, stamps, and basic necessities. A simple way to remember the rule about inflation is to remember that things that man makes go down in price (e.g., manufacturing, building). Things that God makes tend to go up in value wages (e.g., land, food, natural resources).

Now, how does inflation affect the $100,000 in the earlier example? An item a person could buy today for $100,000 with a 3 percent inflation rate will only be worth $97,000 the next year. In 10 years, it would be worth only $76,023; therefore, during a 30-year retirement, $100,000 would be worth only $42,619.

Catastrophic Account

The next account you need is another defensive account. This is the catastrophic account that protects you and your family from things that are out of your control. This would cover the variety of insurance needed — health, dental, life, disability, umbrella, and long-term care. Today, many people have significant concern about health insurance. It is expensive because it is used, and today's premium payment is designed to cover the cost of future treatment. One popular health insurance option to cover catastrophic events is the health savings account (HSA). With an HSA, the covered person pays an annual premium that depends on the size of the household. A portion of the premium buys a high-deductible health care policy to cover major medical expenses such as cancer and heart attacks. The extra premium goes to a savings account that can be used to pay for regular medical visits and minor emergencies, which helps you control your medical expenses. The HSA grows tax deferred and, for medical purposes, is tax free. Another benefit is that the savings account can be passed on year after year so that it can grow to a rather large sum of money over time. It is extremely important to find a health care policy that best fits your needs. If you do not have health insurance, any portfolio that you create or save could be at risk of being lost.

Here is a quiz…which is the most overbought insurance? The reason why this insurance is overbought is because there is a 100 percent probability that it will be used. That's right, it's life insurance. We all will die some day, so we tend to own this investment, but people often buy life insurance without a plan or a strategy. Understanding the different types of life insurance will help you make sound decisions. There are three types of insurance: term insurance, whole life insurance, and variable life insurance.

Term insurance is generally the lowest in cost, but it can be the most expensive if it is never used. Less than 2 percent of term policies ever pay out to beneficiaries. The policies are good for a certain period of time and pay out a fixed benefit. Once the time expires, the policy ends and renewing the policy usually means the premiums increase. If the insured becomes ill during the term, and the policy expires, the insured may not be insurable with another company. Often employers offer term policies as part of a benefits package, and once your job ends, so does the insurance.

If you become uninsurable, there is a risk to your loved ones. When is it a good time to own a term policy? Own one if you need to take care of risk associated with a certain time period, such as paying for college, paying off a mortgage or debt, buying out a partner, or if it is the only policy your cash flow can sustain. You should know before investing in any life insurance policy how much you need to pay for the risk you have. Picking a random death benefit dollar amount may not be enough to cover your family's needs, or you may be paying too much in premiums and not enjoying the use of your money today.

Whole life insurance is what it sounds like. If you make the agreed-upon premium payments to the insurance company, it will insure you for your whole life. As long as the policy is being paid, your heirs will get a payout. Because the insurance company has a high probability of paying out the policy, the premiums are usually fairly high. This type of policy is good to replace the insured person's income stream or to provide for a loved one after you pass away.

Variable whole life is similar to whole life in that as long as the premium payments are made and there are assets in the policy account, then the insurance is in force. If the cash value runs out, the policy lapses and the insurance is not responsible for paying a benefit. Because investment choices are left to the policy owner and risk is reduced to the insurance company, this policy premium can be less expensive than that of a whole life policy. Your risk is that you may not have a policy in the future.

Other mistakes made when purchasing insurance include not understanding all its parts: ownership, beneficiary, insurance, and taxes. The owner is the person or entity who controls of policy. The owner of the policy at the time of death can be responsible for estate taxes or gift taxes. The insured is defined as the person whose death would trigger the insurance company to pay out the policy. The beneficiary is the person receiving the money. A warning: Life insurance beneficiary payouts are currently exempt from income tax. If the insured and the owner are the same, it can cause an estate tax, which can be very expensive. Consult your certified public accountant.

What Type of Insurance Is Overlooked?

Suppose you have legal printing press in your basement, and every day it prints a $100 bill. Would you buy a warranty to replace the income the machine makes every day? More than likely, you would. Almost everyone would buy a warranty to replace the lost income. Disability insurance works much like the warranty to replace lost income. If you cannot perform your job due to illness or disability, the insurance will supplement your income. The risk of becoming disabled is a greater risk to your family than the risk of your death. Being disabled usually adds unaccustomed layers of expense to a household, and, frequently, becoming disabled reduces the household income.

What Type of Insurance Is Underbought?

Umbrella policies protect us from financial extremes that we do not expect or have covered under our current policies. Umbrella policies are reasonably priced and generally provide $1 million to $10 million. You can often add these umbrella policies to your car or homeowners insurance.

What Type of Insurance Is Overpaid?

Long-term care policies are considered to be expensive, but they are expensive because there is a very high probability that you will use the benefits. Long-term care insurance is extremely important to own. The government has a website www.longtermcare.gov to help people make informed decisions about purchasing long-term care policies. Considerations include the amount of benefit, the type of inflation protection (compounding, non-compounding), how to estimate the pool of money and how money is treated with respect to withdrawals and inflation protection, and what triggers the policy to be in force. Something to consider is the amount of benefit you may need and for how long you may need it. How will this pool of money be treated for inflation protection? Should you compound the benefit, use simple interest, or not worry about inflation at all? When you need the policy, what triggers the policy to be in force? Are benefits paid out on a daily, weekly, or monthly rate and what restrictions apply? Some policies may cover home care, assisted living, and/or nursing homes.

A few issues to consider when investing in an insurance policy are the strength and experience of the insurance company. In several cases, insurance companies have raised their premium rates after years of premium payments to a point where the policy owner can no longer afford the policy. Not knowing the insurance company, how your policy works, or that you have invested in the proper riders can be costly.

General Investment Account

The next account is the general investment account (GIA), or the dream account, which would include your college savings account (529 plans and Coverdale individual retirement accounts (IRAs)). Everyone wants to start here without building a base. Many of the same investments in the GIA can be found in an IRA. So, before you seriously fund this account, you need to take advantage of your IRA options.

Start with the real basics of investing. There are three things you can do with your money:

- Hold cash or money market funds.
- Lend your money to get interest paid to you.
- Own things.

A step above holding cash is lending your money to a business, person, or government and getting paid an interest payment; at maturity, your money is returned to you. Lending involves the principal you pay and the interest you expect in return. The lower your risk, the lower the interest rate. The higher your risk, the higher the interest rate. Also, the shorter the maturity, the lower the rate. The longer the loan period, the higher the interest (since you will lose some value to inflation). On a newly issued bond, the coupon is the interest rate being offered. Maturity is when the bond matures. Bond ratings reflect the risk that you may lose your principal. The AAA rating is the safest, so the lower the quality, the higher the risk.

There are several basic types of fixed-income investments. One of the most common is the certificate of deposit (CD). CDs are issued by banks and backed by Federal Deposit Insurance Corporation (FDIC) insurance. Due to the low risk and the usually short term, CD interest rates tend to be low and are taxable as income. Another safe investment is a bond issued by United States government or a government agency that has the implied backing of the federal government. Federal government bonds are exempt from state income tax but not federal income tax. Common government issues include Fannie Maes, Ginnie Maes, Freddie Macs, and TVAs. States, counties, and cities also issue bonds, called municipal bonds. Municipal bonds are usually exempt from federal income tax, so the higher the tax bracket of persons holding municipal bonds, the larger benefit they receive from these investments. Municipal bonds should not be placed in IRA-like accounts since they are already tax efficient. If you are looking for higher interest rates, corporations will also borrow your money. Corporate rates are fully taxable and the quality of the bond is based on the strength of the corporation. Another source of paid interest is insurance companies. They offer bonds or fixed-rate annuities. The fixed annuity grows at a pre-agreed interest rate that is tax deferred; when a person takes out the money, it becomes taxable.

Most people own a home with the expectation that it will increase in value over time. People also own art, companies (stocks), and commodities (oil, gold, currency) with the expectation that they will sell at a price higher than the purchase price. Some of these investments pay out a small income while they appreciate in value. The expected rate of return in these investments, since they are more risky than bonds, is just more than 10 percent over a long period of time. This category is also known as equities.

To reduce the risk of losing your money by concentrating your money in one investment like cash, bonds, or equities, you should consider mutual funds. You pool your money with other people's money to create enough capital to buy a large variety of investments that are managed by a set of rules outlined in a prospectus. Certain fees are removed from the investment pool to pay the professionals involved in managing the assets. However, the investments inside a mutual fund can create uncontrolled taxes and income, which can be a surprise during tax time.

Individual Retirement Account

The investments we discussed above can be held in a general investment account or in an IRA. This leads us to the fourth account a person should have, an IRA. In this chapter "IRA" is used as the default term for any account designed by law for retirement purposes. The well-known retirement accounts include the IRA, Roth IRA, 401(k), Roth 401(k), pension plan, 403(b), SIMPLE IRA, SEP IRA, 401(a). When withdrawing money from a Roth IRA, the income is free from federal income tax. Money from the other retirement plans is subject to income tax upon withdrawal. The use of IRAs to control taxes can be a sophisticated task and should be planned by experts.

After all of these accounts are funded, what do you do next?

Supplemental Retirement Account

Now comes the supplemental retirement account (SRA). If you need more income in retirement annuities (fixed, indexed, or variable), SRAs are good tools. If retirement income is not needed and the goal is to pass on as much as possible to your heirs, then the use of 529 college funding plans or leveraging your estate with life insurance can increase benefits to your heirs. The use of gifting to charities while you're alive is also a great way to supplement your wealth by improving your income tax or capital gains tax rate.

All of these issues are like a sports team in which each position has strengths and weaknesses, and the better you understand the positions, the more success you will have. You are the owner of your wealth; a team of professionals (a financial advisor, a tax expert, and an estate attorney) will be the driving force to help you build a great portfolio. Everyone can succeed at investing by following a few simple rules: pay yourself first, diversify your investments, understand the basics, hire expert financial coaches, and spend more time educating yourself about money than worrying about it.

Chapter 5

Planning for Income Tax Efficiency

Contributing Author John Lau, CFP®, CPA, M.S. (Taxation)

Any one may so arrange his affairs that his taxes shall be as low as possible; he is not bound to choose that pattern which will best pay the Treasury; there is not even a patriotic duty to increase one's taxes[. . .]. Appellate Court Justice Billings Learned Hand, Helvering v. Gregory, 69 F.2d 809, 810-11 (2d Cir. 1934).

Tax considerations are normally an important factor but not the driving force behind most financial planning strategies. Instead, factors such as age, financial situation, risk tolerance, investment time frame, and suitability are likely to be more significant in selecting a particular portfolio mix. In addition, an overriding investment strategy for a retiree in need of funds is structuring a portfolio that generates a steady cash flow.

Once an investment plan is determined, an advisor can help enhance returns and profits by recommending tax-efficient strategies to carry out the plan. This includes analyzing the tax effects of various investment options. Knowing the tax effects of, and the tax planning opportunities for, particular investments is important when implementing a financial plan. In some cases, the underlying tax implications will lead an investor to choose one investment over another.

While tax avoidance is certainly illegal, you should plan your financial affairs for tax savings. This is especially important after retirement. You know the old saying "a penny saved is a penny earned." By the same token, a tax dollar saved is an extra dollar to sustain your retirement lifestyle. Although tax planning strategies are as expansive and varied as individuals' circumstances, certain tax attributes are present in a conceptual framework for efficient post-retirement tax planning. Use the framework as a planning checklist with your tax and financial advisors.

1. Why pay taxes on income you don't currently need?

Most of us wouldn't consciously pay more taxes than we have to. But many end up doing just that, year in and year out. The general assumption that somehow we pay less tax after retirement is a myth. Many retirees end up with just as much if not more income after retirement — with post-retirement income from pension income, interest and dividend income, income from rental properties, social security benefits, individual retirement account (IRA) withdrawals, and similar sources. On the other hand, retirees tend to have fewer tax deductions. For one thing, most retirees have their home mortgages already paid off. Without the mortgage interest deduction, they do not have enough to qualify for itemized deductions. Consequently, they take standard deductions and end up paying just as much in taxes (if not more) than before they retired.

Relax! Just because you can no longer itemize deductions, not all hope is lost. Tax planning goes beyond mere deductions. While having legitimate deductions does help, their role in tax savings is overemphasized. One thing you really shouldn't do though is to create deductions just to have deductions. Some retirees even suggest borrowing against their homes for investment. That is a big no-no. Not only would it expose your finances to market volatility and unnecessary risks, you may not be able to deduct the interest because of deduction limitations.

So, what else can you do to save taxes besides tax deductions? A better alternative would be to plan on the income side of the equation.

John and Mary Example

John and Mary are both retired and in their sixties. Their 2006 income and expenses are as follows:

Interest Income		$15,000
Dividend Income		8,000
Capital Gains Distribution[1]		25,000
Pensions and Annuities:		
John	$30,000	
Mary	10,000	40,000
Net Rental Income	$10,000	
Depreciation Expense	- 1,700	8,300
Social Security Income	$27,000	
Nontaxable Portion	- 4,050	22,950
Adjusted Gross Income (AGI)		$119,250

---

[1] Capital gain distributions are typical from mutual fund investments. This may be planned down with mutual funds with low turnover rates, tax-efficient mutual funds, or the use of a money-manager platform so strategies such as wash sales and loss harvesting may be implemented for better tax efficiency.

Since their house is paid for, John and Mary do not have enough deductions to itemize, so they take standard deductions.

Their income tax liabilities are as follows:

Federal	$15,764
State (California)	4,228
	$19,992

John and Mary have a $6,000-a-month lifestyle (or $72,000 a year). Since they don't have a mortgage on the house, they can live quite well on $6,000 a month, and that is including vacation money, eating out, and other entertainment, but excluding taxes.

According to the principle of paying taxes only on needed income, John and Mary could be overpaying taxes on $47,250 of the income that is not currently needed ($119,250 - $72,000 = $47,250). This is the first clue that maybe there are some tax-saving planning options to consider.

Now take a closer look at John and Mary's income picture. Cash flows from pensions, social security, and rental are as follows:

John's pension	$30,000
Mary's pension	10,000
Social security benefits	27,000
Net rental income	10,000
	$77,000

Income from these sources are before interest, dividend, and capital gains, and they total $77,000, an amount that exceeds what John and Mary need every year.

If their investment income can somehow be "planned away" for tax reporting purposes, John and Mary could potentially save more than $12,000 a year:

	Current Tax Returns	Proforma Tax Returns
John's pension	$30,000	$30,000
Mary's pension	10,000	10,000
Net rental income	8,300	8,300
Social security benefits	22,950	21,130
Interest income	15,000	0
Dividend income	8,000	0
Capital gain distrib	25,000	0
	$119,250	$69,430
Federal income tax	15,764	7,089
CA income tax	4,228	675
	$19,992	$ 7,764

This is a total tax savings of $12,228 ($19,992 - $7,764).

John and Mary could have gone on an extra cruise with this savings. The question is: How many cruises have John and Mary missed?

How Many Cruises Have You Been Missing?

Ask your advisor to do an adjusted gross income (AGI) efficiency test for you.

1.   Prepare a monthly retirement expenditure budget.

2.   Compare your annual retirement expenditures with the AGI amount on your tax returns, adjusting for extraordinary items that you don't expect to repeat.

3.   If the figure from 2. is more than 10 percent of your figure from 1., ask your advisor to identify the income items that may potentially be planned away using the planning attributes discussed in this chapter.

Income "Realized" vs. Income "Recognized" (the Timing Attribute)

The John and Mary example illustrates how the *timing* attribute can be effectively considered in tax planning. In [tax] law, there is a difference between income "realized" and income recognized." While income realized means income earned to which you are entitled, income "recognized" addresses *when* that income is reportable for tax purposes. An IRA and a company retirement account are classic examples of the concept between income realization and income recognition. While interest, dividends, and capital gains may continue to accrue in a retirement account (income realization), they are not subject to taxation, and therefore not recognized, until money is withdrawn from these accounts. This income deferral feature is the key reason why IRAs and company retirement accounts remain among the highest value assets owned by retirees outside of their homes and other real estate holdings.

What To Do

Take full advantage of planning with the timing attribute. Ask your advisor to review your tax returns for income items that may be planned away. Common planning alternatives include:

a. Planning for tax-exempt income. This would typically be tax-exempt municipal bonds. Muni bond interest income is generally exempt from federal income tax. Interest income from bonds issued by local and state governments are usually tax-exempt to the issuing state's residents. However, watch out for adjustments for alternative minimum tax with interest income from private activity muni bonds.

b. Planning for tax-deferred income. Tax-deferred annuities may be quite effective for tax deferral purposes. Earnings on these accounts are exempt from income taxation as long as they stay in the account. Income tax is triggered when withdrawals are made. Annuities typically have higher mortality and expense ratios. However, they also provide guarantee features that do not come with conventional investments. One must weigh between the benefits of guarantees and tax deferral against higher mortality and expense ratios.

c. Other tax-advantaged investments. There are alternative investments that are tax advantaged, meaning their income is at least partially sheltered (e.g., by depreciation expense, special tax legislation). Ask your financial advisor about tax-advantaged alternative investments. Examples include royalty income programs, real estate investment trusts (REITs), intangible drilling cost programs, and equipment leasing.

Not All Income Is Taxed the Same (the Characterization Attribute)

Income may be of such different types as capital gains, ordinary income, passive activity income, and portfolio income. Contrary to common belief, not all income is taxed the same. For instance, capital gains are taxed at the maximum federal rate of 15 percent, while ordinary income can be taxed as high as 35 percent. While losses from passive activities may be deducted from passive activity income, they may not be used against non-passive activity income. While capital losses may be used against capital gains, only up to $3,000 of capital losses in any given year may be used against non-capital gain income. If you have a large capital loss carryover and fail to plan for its disposition, it may take a long time to use it up. Any unused capital loss remaining at death is permanently lost. In planning for income tax savings, your advisor should be able to help re-characterize your income to your best advantage.

Refer to the examples below to see how the characterization attribute are used to benefit taxpayers.

LeRoy and Eunice Example

LeRoy and Eunice are retired. Their tax return shows a large investment interest expense carryover (investment interest expense is deductible only to the extent of investment income). In 2007, LeRoy and Eunice sat down with their tax/financial advisors for some planning and decided to sell some of their stocks and reposition their account to a more conservative portfolio. Many of their holdings have low cost basis because they were purchased some years back, and there would be large capital gains if these holdings were sold. LeRoy and Eunice don't have any capital loss carryover to use against the capital gains.

Their advisor suggested a simple tax election to characterize the capital gains from stock sales to ordinary investment income. By doing this, the capital gains from stock sales are fully offset by the suspended investment interest carryover, resulting in no or very little income tax on the sale of their equity holdings.

Renee Example

Renee is retired, and she has a rental house that she wants to sell. She has owned the property for 15 years, and the real estate has substantially appreciated in value. Renee wants to get out of the landlord business and to spend more time traveling and visiting her grandchildren. However, the rental has a low income tax basis and potentially high built-in capital gains if the property is sold. Renee wants to know how she may sell the property with minimum income tax exposure.

One obvious alternative would be to consider a tax-deferred "like kind" exchange under section 1031 of the Internal Revenue Code (IRC). But this would limit Renee's options. Under 1031, Renee would have to replace the "relinquishment" property with a like kind "replacement" property – essentially real estate for real estate. Renee wonders if there are other options.

Renee's advisor looked through her tax returns and noticed capital loss carryover from prior stock sales as well as passive activity loss suspended from prior years. Between the two losses, Renee may shelter about 90 percent of the capital gains from taxes. The other 10 percent of the gains is taxed at the 15 percent federal rate. Renee is perfectly happy to pay the 15 percent tax.

Result: Renee sold her rental property, invested the proceeds in a portfolio mix with complete liquidity and accessibility, and no longer has the headaches associated with being a landlord.

What to do

Your advisor is there to help you plan ahead to minimize the cost of taxation. Before you embark on any major capital transactions, meet with your advisor to crunch the numbers. A good advisor can save you a fistful of dollars.

Consult with your advisor if you contemplate any of the following capital transactions:

- Sale of real estate. Planning considerations include IRC 1031 like kind exchange, installment sale, suspended losses, and capital loss carryovers.
- Sale of business. Planning consideration includes the allocation of sale price to components most advantageous to your tax situation. Special tax considerations apply for related-party transactions.
- Exercising stock options. Beware of the alternative minimum tax (AMT) trap.
- Tax planning with stocks and bonds (e.g., preserving stock losses by avoiding the wash sale rules).
- Changing employment. Should you or shouldn't you roll over your 401(k) plan?
- Having a baby, or becoming a grandparent. Consider education funding and estate planning opportunities.

When in doubt, see your advisor. Many good advisors are underutilized. Get them to help you improve your financial situation.

Chapter 6

Investing for Growth and Income with Stocks and Bonds

Contributing Author C.J. Liepman

Are Stocks and Bonds Right for You?

Investor's with $100,000 or more can now consider the services of a private investment manager who specializes in stocks and bonds to help them construct and manage their personal investment portfolio.

What follows describes a disciplined process for constructing and managing personalized stock and bond portfolios. This process works best for investors with a need to control how they select investments and what they will do with their investments as conditions change. This process enables investors to own and manage their portfolio for the rest of their investment lives, with the aid of their private investment manager.

First Step – Know Yourself/Know Your Advisor

The first step for every investor is to get help. A professional investment manager with experience in managing stock and bond portfolios should be consulted when considering this approach. Investment styles can vary greatly between managers, making your choice of a manager who matches your beliefs and your tolerances a very important part of your investment success.

Step two is to gain a full understanding of your investment goals and future financial needs. Your life is unique and therefore your investment choices are unique. Custom-fitting your portfolio to your life is one of the greatest benefits to constructing a personalized portfolio. Consulting with an independent professional adds an objective perspective to your investment plan.

The understanding gained from a formal review of your financial situation enables you and your investment manager to develop an appropriate role for stocks and bonds in your portfolio and to develop an investment process and discipline that works for you. *Note:* When we speak of investment managers, we are talking about Registered Investment Advisors who accept discretionary authority over your assets and have accepted a fiduciary liability to you. These individuals are Investment Advisors (series 65 and 66 licensed) in addition to holding other licenses. What this means to you is that they are bound by their fiduciary liability to always do what is in your best interests and to put their personal interests aside. This is a fundamental distinction from those professionals whose performance and continued employment is based on how they perform for their employers and not their clients.

There Is No Hurry

It is rarely wise to invest a lump sum in the stock market or even the bond market. These markets are always in a state of flux. This is one of the first potentially big mistakes to avoid. The problem for most investors is that they generally bring their money to the stock market at the top of the current cycle and to the bond market at the bottom.

To avoid this mistake, seek an advisor who is neither motivated by commissions nor compensated independently of your results. Your advisors should be compensated on the basis of your performance. The more they make for you, the more they make for themselves.

Working from the Bottom Up

Start by investing in money market funds, then seek stocks or bonds only when they are exceeding the return of money market funds by a reasonable margin and have excellent prospects for continuing this performance in the foreseeable future. This approach first compares the potential return of an individual stock or bond investment with the relatively risk-free return of a money market fund. After all, if you're investing in stocks or bonds, you should get a better return over the foreseeable future than from money market funds.

If the economy is worsening and interest rates have peaked, then bonds may offer the best alternative to stocks or money market funds for the foreseeable future.

If the economy is strengthening and interest rates are low, then stocks may offer the best alternative to bonds or money markets.

Having the flexibility within your investment discipline to move your money between these three major asset classes without undue cost is fundamental to your investment success. Knowing your role in decision making and that of your investment manager is also just as important to your success.

No Trade or Not to Trade

Assuming you have chosen to invest in stocks and have found a stock with good growth and return prospects, you should understand the difference between trading and investing. If you think that you can make some money on a stock in the short term, then you are a stock trader. Simply put, stock trading is a form of gambling. The outcome of most stock trading is either a small gain or a small loss. Sometimes, a large gain or a large loss can be experienced overnight with news of an acquisition, serious lawsuit, change in leadership, or other serious event. Emotion usually plays a role in stock trading and drives many traders to make poorly timed decisions. Stock traders must make many trades (or gambles) over time and typically have many trades going at the same time. Just like gambling, the odds are against long-term success in stock trading for the majority of the investing public.

Investing for Life

So, how do you avoid gambling with stocks and instead invest in good companies for long-term wealth building? Well, you have to consider that your investment life is going to be a very long one. Therefore, your investments should also be for very long periods of time. While investing in cash equivalents can protect purchasing power and portfolio value in the short term, cash equivalents do not add to purchasing power significantly over time. Higher yielding bonds can add both to purchasing power and to portfolio value in the long term if they are bought when their yields are as good as or better than stocks.

History has shown that the additional risk of investing in stocks can add future purchasing power to your investment dollar and thus help you to build wealth over the span of many years.

The Companies You Keep – It's Fundamental

Selecting companies with the financial strength to prosper in good times and bad is an elemental part of this investment process. This is where the study of company fundamentals plays a very important part in the investment process.

Unfortunately, this is where simplicity ends and complicated formulas for determining the fair or intrinsic share value of a company come into play. Every money manager uses formulas for the valuation of various kinds of companies. A company that is growing quickly but not yet making a profit is valued differently than a stable company that pays a growing dividend. Some companies are seasonal in nature and some are highly diversified in their businesses.

Developing Your Investment Discipline

Assuming that you have selected a number of stocks worthy of your investment dollars, how much of each is appropriate for your portfolio? Studies have shown that a minimum investment of 3 percent to 4 percent is enough for an individual stock to make a positive impact on your portfolio but not so much that an ill-timed investment would hurt overall performance. Studies on diversification have also shown that no more than 10 percent of your portfolio should be allocated to an individual stock. Modern portfolio theory holds that 25 percent is the maximum that should be allocated to any one industry sector. A good way to think about diversification is to think in terms of balance. Maintaining a properly diversified balance of individual stock positions without concentrating too much in any one industry will help to smooth your returns over time and maintain broad participation across the investment landscape.

These self-imposed rules are the beginning of your investment discipline. If you believe that you want to reduce risk by maximizing diversification, then start with a 3 percent position per stock and seek to invest in 33 stocks over time with no more than an 11 percent exposure to any one of the nine major industry sectors.

Pie Chart Anyone?

Members of the investment management profession use charts to demonstrate the degree of diversification that has been achieved within a portfolio. These charts come in several varieties. The same portfolio can be visualized by industry segment, investment style, capitalization of companies, and geographical diversity, as the following charts show.

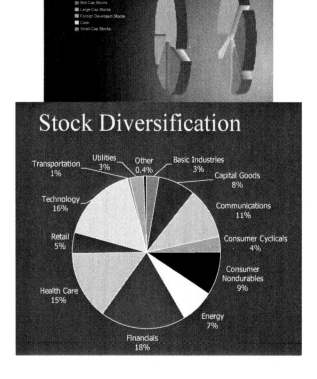

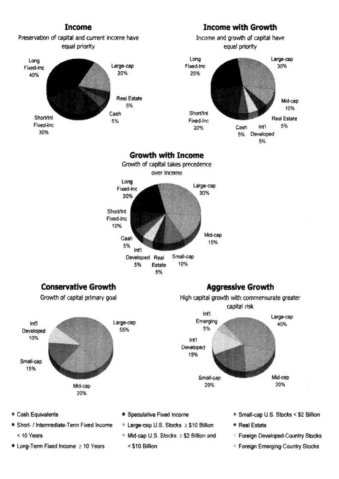

What Next?

To this point we have discussed the first parts of constructing an investment discipline. Once you have begun to make investments, you must develop discipline for what happens next. Some stocks will go up in price and become a larger part of your overall portfolio while others may go down in price. A well-diversified portfolio will have some areas that do very well and some that do very poorly for a time. Knowing how to realize profits and what to do with unrealized losses is important to managing a well-diversified portfolio.

Discipline Matters

What if you buy a great company that has done a great job for shareholders in the past just before that company or the economy runs into hard times? Our advice is to stick with your decision to own that company long term and take advantage of the drop in share price in a disciplined manner. Studies have shown that when this happens, it works out to the investor's advantage to increase ownership in this stock up to 10 percent of the portfolio. Patience is your friend in this discipline. Allowing the price to drop 30 percent before buying another position for your portfolio and then even another 30 percent will usually allow you to capture the lowest price this stock will trade at during even the toughest economic declines. The math on two 30 percent drops in price produces an overall drop of 50 percent in share price.

The following chart shows what happened to McDonalds' stock price from June 2000 through June 2007. This is an actual demonstration of our discipline and the resulting return from this stock.

1. First Profit Taken at $20 per share by selling 50 shares for $1,000
2. Second Profit Taken at $26.60 by selling 38 shares for $1,000
3. Third Profit Taken at $35.38 by selling 28 shares for $1,000
4. Fourth Profit Taken at $47 by selling 21 shares for $1,000
5. Remaining shares equals 63 worth $3,000 +

Our discipline is to choose high-quality companies whose growth and earnings exceed the return of money markets and bonds for the previous 10 years and which, at the time of purchase, were fairly valued toward the lower end of their valuation ranges. In the year 2000, as the tech bubble was bursting, a fair price for MCD was $30 per share and it was bought. Because of the mad cow disease scare and the general economic decline, the price of MCD shares subsequently fell more than 50 percent from the point of purchase. Instead of taking real losses, our discipline dictated the purchase of another $3,000 worth of stock each time the price fell by 30 percent. There were three total purchases made of MCD over a year and a half as the recession bottomed out. At its lowest purchase price, our portfolio had its maximum allocation of MCD, which was nearly 10 percent of the portfolio. During this time, the dividend yield from MCD was higher than money market funds. Each purchase promised a better yield than money market funds or bonds. As the share price of MCD recovered along with the economy, we sold off the higher cost lots (purchase prices). While this recovery was happening, we also realized profits from our purchase of $15 per share by "rebalancing" this position every time it grew by 33 percent ($4,000 to $3,000).

The net result of managing our original $3,000 investment in McDonalds has been a realized profit of $4,000 to date, plus dividends (which were paying more than money markets at the time of purchase). We still currently own more than $3,000 in the stock, with an unrealized profit of more than $2,300.

Simply put:

QUALITY + DISCIPLINE + PATIENCE = PROFITS

There are many real examples of how this discipline has worked over time.

Doing Your Homework

How do you avoid losing money in the stock market? The short answer is that you can't avoid the temporary loss of money in the stock market or any other market for that matter. Without going into a lengthy explanation, just about every purchase of an equity or bond involves the immediate loss of some money (investment cost). The better question may be: What protective measures can be taken when purchasing equities and bonds?

Waiting for companies or bonds to become a good value can be the first step to loss avoidance. Valuation work is a risk reduction technique that prices a company's shares independently of how they are currently priced in the market. This work generally attempts to place a fair value range of prices on the company given the flexibility of variables affecting price during normal economic conditions. If the price of the stock is too high, purchase should be avoided. If the price of the stock is below the low end, a serious look at factors creating this condition should be evaluated before the purchase is made.

Valuation work is not the only technique for protecting your principal. Insurance can be purchased along with an equity purchase in the form of a put option. This technique is known as hedging. Just like insuring your home with a deductible, there is a known loss in the form of the periodic premium as a trade-off against a potential disaster. As the price of your equity moves up and down, your overall value won't change very much because of the hedging aspect. If your long equity position has gained significant value during your option period, your option can be allowed to expire, thus revealing your net gains on your account statements. If you wish to continue hedging your position, you can purchase a new put option for another period of time. Our MCD example of how our discipline performed did not use the put option as a protection against the loss of account value during the economic decline. A covered put LEAP option on the first purchase would have protected account value while our discipline achieved the goal of finding the lowest trading price for the stock and ultimately gaining profits. When MCD traded at $21 per share, we would have put our first purchase to a new owner at the original price we paid and closed the put option. The net effect of this transaction would have been to recover our original investment much sooner and to free up capital to reinvest into the stock at a lower price. Considering that the purchase of covered puts costs a minimum of 6 percent of the investment per year, we feel this option is too costly to employ as an ongoing portfolio management technique.

Now That We've Made All This Money

As mentioned in our discussion of discipline, we continue to take profits as our stock prices go up to rebalance the stock position. Ultimately, there will be a reversal of the trend the next time our economy falters. What position will your portfolio be in at the top of such a market? How will you deal with the ensuing decline of the economy and of the prices of your stocks? What will your cash position look like at the top of the market? What will you do with your cash as the market declines? How will you protect the value and profits of your current stock positions? These are very real concerns.

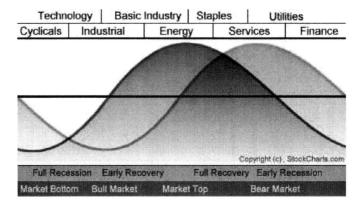

Technology		Basic Industry	Staples		Utilities
Cyclicals	Industrial	Energy		Services	Finance

Copyright (c), StockCharts.com

Full Recession	Early Recovery		Full Recovery	Early Recession
Market Bottom	Bull Market	Market Top		Bear Market

Throughout history, our economy has moved through cycles of prosperity and recession. Managing stock and bond portfolios requires adaptation to these cycles to mitigate their damaging effects while taking full advantage of the upside opportunities. Recognition of the current state of the economy and the ensuing transitions to subsequent stages is the role of the economist. Much like weathercasters, economists can easily tell what the economy was doing in the recent past but differ in their opinions about the future. The most difficult characteristic of cycle changes is to determine how long each phase might last.

After our portfolio made it through the last economic decline with no realized losses and recovered ahead of the Dow Jones Industrial Index and long ahead of the S&P 500 and Nasdaq indexes, we began to consider the impact of a long bull market. Real value opportunities have begun to diminish as most stocks have achieved full valuation. While this has brought with it many profit-taking opportunities, cash has begun to accumulate in our portfolios as new valuation-based opportunities have subsided. Our concerns have been that the difference between the forward-looking returns of stocks vs. bonds is diminishing and the returns of stocks over bonds look less attractive going forward. Having been here before, we look at the current condition of the capital markets as precarious given the world economic situation. Therefore, we are slow to invest new money into the current market, which we believe is primed for a reversal.

Consider that bond values diminish as interest rates climb. We are faced with a conundrum of where to invest money as the markets top out and parity develops between stock and bond returns. At this point, we know that something will give and that we may be stuck in a trading range for some time without a definitive direction of where to go with our money market funds. Our primary concern during a time like this would be to use the technique of progressive hedging on a portfolio-wide basis using recently developed exchange-traded funds. Remember that longer bonds become a good hedge against diminishing stock prices only as interest rates fall. If interest rates are climbing and there is parity between bond and stock yields, then we look to invest in higher short-term yields so that we don't suffer portfolio decline from both bond prices and stock prices during this period. Money market funds capture the majority of short-term yield in bonds but do not change in price. This is protective to the account value during these transition periods. Should bonds develop yields in excess of long-term stock yields, then they become a wise investment for long-term appreciation. During a period of dropping interest rates, bonds in your portfolio will gain in value.

Other than hedging the portfolio, we will hold to our selection and management disciplines using our cash position to purchase new lots of stock as prices decline. The portfolio will outperform the broad markets as it will decline at a slower rate, but without hedging or wholesale abandonment, there must be an expectation of temporary decline and repositioning of the portfolio into a lower cost basis.

How Are You Doing?

Below is an example of an actual portfolio that went through this process during the last market decline from 2002 through 2004. That decline was the second worst since the Great Depression. As you will note, the portfolio did decline in value by 15 percent over a two-year period. However, this decline was less pronounced than the decline of the S&P 500, which declined by 25 percent during the same period. The worst decline during this period was 20 percent for our portfolio, while the S&P 500 lost a maximum of 30 percent. In addition, our portfolio recovered sooner and kept up with the eventual rise in the S&P 500. The difference in the experience of our portfolio and the S&P 500 was that we started with a great deal of cash because of previous profit taking and were making larger investments in recovering stocks, bringing our investments back sooner as well as doing so with less portfolio risk than the S&P 500. Finally, while the S&P 500 did not fully recover until the end of 2004, our portfolio had reached this point a full year and three months earlier.

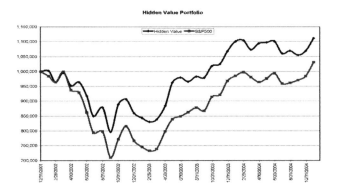

What About Bonds?

We have not discussed bonds up to this point other than to point to them as a useful hedge against declining portfolio values during times of market decline and decreasing interest rates.

For the retired family, bonds are very useful for meeting the daily needs of the family with enough stocks (typically 30 percent) in the portfolio to overcome the effects of inflation. Typically, these portfolios are no longer growth oriented but are principal and income oriented. Families in retirement no longer produce savings and can no longer replace money lost during a stock market decline. Retired families should rely on the interest income from their bonds to meet their living expenses and not from the growth of their stock portfolio. From the outset of this discussion about stocks and bonds, we have built our case for stocks only when stocks provide a more attractive future return potential than bonds. When this is no longer the case, then money market funds or short- to intermediate-term high-quality bonds become the better choice for real returns.

Chapter 7

Ten Exit Strategies for Highly Appreciated Real Estate

Contributing Author Larry Weiss, CPA, CSA

As a CPA and financial advisor, I work with many clients who have an enviable real estate problem. They bought rental property 20 to 30 years ago. They work hard to maintain their property and have good relationships with their tenants. Many bought their properties for approximately $150,000. Now they find their property to be worth more than $1,150,000.

The time had come to sell their property. As clients approach retirement, they want to benefit from the equity in their investment real estate. Over the years many clients have come to me wishing to sell their property, but without paying all the taxes immediately, either in the taxable year of sale or by the following April 15. Most people want to consider different sales options to understand the tax consequences of each and to see which strategy best suits their needs without resulting in hundreds of thousand of dollars in taxes due. Careful planning is essential to making the right decision.

So clients ask, "What is the best way for me to dispose of my property without being clobbered by taxation?" The answer depends on the individual clients' needs and their complete financial picture.

First, determine whether a property is an investment property or a personal residence. Investment property and personal residences face different taxation under the Internal Revenue Code.

There are 10 different alternatives to paying immediate capital gains taxes from the sale of property. Let's start with investment property.

An Investment Property Example

Assume clients bought a property for $150,000 more than 20 years ago. Today the property is worth $1,150,000. The taxpayers have deducted $100,000 in past depreciation expenses. They have decided to sell the property and want to understand the tax consequences of their sale:

Federal Taxes

Depreciation Recapture	25%	$25,000
Capital Gain Taxes	15%	150,000
Total Federal Taxes		175,000

California Taxes

Income Taxes	9.3%	102,300

Total Estimated Taxes
$277,300

Thus, the tax rate from the sale of this property is approaching 28 percent. Other tax rates may apply or tax deductions may be affected by alternative minimum tax (AMT) considerations.

More than one client has asked "What are my options and what is the tax pain?"

1. Getting a step up in tax basis

This is best described as a timing strategy.

Assume that Joan and Larry want to sell their rental property only after one of them dies. When a taxpayer, say Larry, dies, his assets are valued at the date of death or at an alternative value six months after his death. This value establishes the new tax cost basis for determining the gain or loss.

Also assume that Larry and Joan bought property many years ago for $100,000, but the value of the property at Larry's death is $500,000. Joan can potentially sell that property after Larry's death for $500,000 and pay no income or capital gains taxes from the sale.

An important consideration is the titling of the property. In above example, if Joan and Larry hold the real estate as community property with rights of survivorship, then the whole property receives a step up in basis at Larry's death.

If the property is held as a joint tenancy, only Larry's share of the basis receives a step up in basis.

Example:

Joan and Larry hold title to their property as joint tenants. Larry dies. The step up in cost basis only applies to his share of the property. Joan's basis remains the same as before:

Larry's half of the property

(50% of fair market value (FMV)
at date of death) $250,000

Joan's half of the property $ 50,000

Cost basis of property after Larry's death $300,000

Under joint tenancy with rights of survivorship, when Joan sells the property for $500,000, she has a taxable gain of $200,000 (FMV at death = $500,000 minus the new basis $300,000).

If the property is held as community property, the entire property receives a step up in basis to $500,000 and Joan can sell the property without taxation.

2. Converting a rental property to a personal residence

Under IRC section 121 taxpayers may exclude part of their gain from the sale of their personal residence.

To qualify for this tax treatment the property must qualify under the "ownership" test and "personal use" test. The taxpayer must have owned the property at least two of the last five years and used the property as a personal residence for at least two of the last five years. The taxpayer may exclude $250,000 of gain if the taxpayer is single and $500,000 if the taxpayer is married and files jointly.

The IRS only requires taxes to be paid on any depreciation taken after May 6, 1997.

Example:

Let's say Ann and Henry, a married couple, own a single-family rental property that they plan to sell. They bought the house 11 years ago for $100,000 and have taken $25,000 in depreciation expense over the years on their tax returns. They can now sell their property for $500,000. If Ann and Henry move into the home and establish this house as their personal residence for two years, they can exclude up to a $500,000 gain from taxation. Their accountant has advised them that $23,000 of depreciation has been taken after May 6, 1997. Thus, Ann and Henry can sell their property and only pay taxes on $23,000, which is a relatively small amount compared to the $425,000 gain.

Ann and Henry have future planning opportunities. The section 121 exclusion can be used every two years. So, with proper planning, a couple can use this exclusion every two years on a different property they own. Section 121(d)(10) does require that the taxpayer own qualifying property for at least five years after acquiring it in a section 1031 exchange.

3. Having your cake and eating it too (Using IRC section 121 and 1031 on the same property)

A taxpayer may now exclude $250,000 ($500,000 for certain joint filers) under section 121 of capital gains realized, and defer other capital gains through a 1031 exchange on a single property. The new procedure applies to homeowners who use their property as their personal residence and also use the property for "investment business purposes." Investment business purposes can include a home office or rental of a portion of the property.

Examples:

1) Personal Residence/Rental Property

Fred and Wilma have converted their personal residence to a rental property in recent years. IRC section 121 requires a taxpayer to live in the residence in two of the last five years to be eligible for the capital gains exclusion. Thus, by converting their home to a rental property, Fred and Wilma may take advantage of the section 121 capital gains exclusion and the 1031 tax-deferred exchange.

2) Combination Property

Barney and Betty own a property that includes their personal residence and another unit held for business purposes. Part of the property is eligible for capital gains exclusion and the other structure is eligible for capital gains tax deferral. A simple example is a property with a home and guesthouse. The rented guesthouse constitutes a property held for business purposes. Each component is accounted for as a separate property in an exchange. The home would be eligible for section 121 treatment and the guesthouse could use section 1031.

3) Dual-use Property

Bam Bam and Pebbles own a house that constitutes a single dwelling unit. In an example from the IRS, 2/3 of the home is used as a personal residence and 1/3 as an office in the taxpayer's trade or business. A dual-use property can benefit from both the capital gains exclusion and the capital gains deferral.

The History

In the past, most properties were classified as either personal residences eligible for capital gains exclusion treatment or investment properties eligible for 1031 exchange transactions. Properties were rarely eligible to take advantage of both section 121 and section 1031 exchanges simultaneously. The IRS Revenue Procedure 2005-14 has expanded the opportunities to use both section 121 and section 1031 in one transaction.

Section 1031 Exchanges

Taxpayers owning investment property for business purposes have been able to defer the capital gains taxes through a 1031 exchange. Under IRC section 1031, a property can be sold and "replaced" by another property that is "like kind." By using careful planning and following the proper steps, a taxpayer may defer the income taxes due from the disposition of the property.

Section 121 Capital Gains Exclusion

Taxpayers may exclude the gain realized on the sale or exchange of their principal residence if the property was owned and used as the taxpayers' principal residence for at least two years during the five years ending with the date of sale. The exclusion amount is limited to $500,000 for married filing joint returns and $250,000 for others.

Example 1: Receiving Cash in the Exchange

Assume Joe and Sylvia live in Los Altos. They bought their home 15 years ago for $350,000. They lived on this property until 2003 when they rented the property to tenants, thereby converting their personal residence into a business property. They have taken cumulative depreciation deductions of $25,000 on their income tax returns. In 2005, Joe and Sylvia decided it was time to sell their property. Joe and Sylvia exchanged their property for a condo worth $700,000 and $500,000 in cash. Joe and Sylvia continue to rent their condo to tenants. This property continues to be used for "business purposes." This 1031 exchange can use the capital gains exclusion under section 121 because for two of the last five years Joe and Sylvia lived on the property.

The Results:

Amount Realized	$1,200,000
Less Adjusted Basis (cost less depreciation)	<u>325,000</u>
Realized Gain	875,000
Less: Gain excluded under section 121	<u>500,000</u>
Gain deferred under section 1031	$ 375,000

In this illustration, under section 121, Joe and Sylvia are allowed to exclude up to $500,000 from the sale of their residence. The couple can also defer the remaining gain through the 1031 exchange process. So, Joe and Sylvia can keep the $500,000 in cash (boot) free of capital gains tax and defer the remaining gain through the 1031 exchange.

Joe and Sylvia's basis in the new property is $325,000, which is equal to the basis of the relinquished property at the time of the exchange ($325,000), increased by the gain excluded under section 121($500,000), and reduced by the cash received by Joe and Sylvia ($500,000).

Example 2: Increase Tax Basis on New Property

Assume Joe and Sylvia complete a 1031 exchange based on the facts previously described. The only difference is that Joe and Sylvia exchange into a condo worth $1,200,000. The condo continues to be rented to tenants and held for business purposes. Joe and Sylvia receive no cash in the transaction.

The Results:

Amount Realized	$1,200,000
Less Adjusted Basis (cost less depreciation)	325,000
Realized Gain	875,000
Less: Gain excluded under section 121	500,000
Gain deferred under section 1031	$ 375,000

Joe and Sylvia's basis in the new property is $ 825,000, which is equal to the basis of the relinquished property, $325,000 at the time of the exchange, increased by the gain excluded under section 121 ($500,000), and reduced by the cash received. Since Joe and Sylvia did not receive any cash, the new basis has increased dramatically.

Great appreciation in real estate has provided unique planning opportunities for people who own property with business and residential purposes. Revenue Procedure 2005-14 provides six different examples. Careful consideration to each individual's circumstances and tax needs is essential.

4. 1031 Exchanges

An active, thriving real estate market has been essential to the overall health of the American economy. To help promote this environment, Congress established the ability for taxpayers to buy and sell properties while deferring taxation.

Properties that are held for investment purposes or in a trade or business are eligible for a tax deferral 1031 exchange. The taxpayers' personal residence is not eligible. The sale of the property (relinquished property) and the purchase of the new property (replacement property) must be "like kind property" and follow all the rules to qualify for tax deferral.

When selling the property, the taxpayer must enter into a tax-deferred exchange agreement with a qualified intermediary. The qualified intermediary, also known as an accommodator, holds the proceeds from the sale of the property while the taxpayer looks for a replacement property.

Assume Johnny wants to make a 1031 exchange. He first lists the property to sell. A buyer is found with terms agreed upon, and a contract to sell the property is executed. Accommodation language is part of the contract securing the buyer's cooperation with Johnny's intent to make a 1031 exchange. At closing, the services of a qualified intermediary are arranged to permit the intermediary to become the substitute seller in the transaction. At the close of escrow, all the sales proceeds are sent to the qualified intermediary for safekeeping. Johnny cannot touch the funds and has no rights to those funds until the exchange is complete.

It is essential to select the right qualified intermediary. The qualified intermediary industry is unregulated. Johnny must safeguard the funds and choose a qualified intermediary that has substantial assets and that is bonded to ensure that the funds are safe. In recent months, a few intermediaries did not safeguard such funds and taxpayers' money was lost while being held by an accommodator. This would result in Johnny losing his funds, a failed 1031 exchange, and exposure to capital gains taxes on the failed transaction. Johnny should have used a recommended intermediary such as First American Exchange Company to safeguard his money because of their excellent financial security and technical understanding of the 1031 exchange rules.

Timing is essential when locating the appropriate replacement property. Identification of the replacement property must be completed in writing and signed by Johnny within 45 days of the closing sale of the relinquished property. The identification must contain an unambiguous description of the replacement property. More than one property can be identified under these rules:

Three Property Rule - Identify up to three properties of any value.

200 Percent Rule - Identify more than three properties as long as the total value of the replacement property does not exceed 200 percent of the relinquished property.

95 Percent Rule - There is no limit as to the total (aggregate) number or value of identified like kind replacement properties permitted under the 95 percent exception as long as you actually acquire and close on 95 percent of the value identified.

Remember, the taxpayer also must complete the purchase of the replacement property by the 180th day after the closing of the relinquished property or by the due date of the taxpayer's income tax return, whichever is sooner.

Example

Let's say Fred's relinquished property closes on December 1. Fred is required to complete the purchase of the replacement property by May 29. But since Fred's income tax return is due April 15, he must complete his replacement purchase by that date or file an extension for his tax return. If Fred completes his tax return by April 15 without finishing the purchase of his replacement property, he has lost the ability to defer his taxes from the sale of the property. The simple solution is to get an income tax extension and complete the purchase of the replacement property within the 180-day limitation. After the replacement purchase is complete, Fred can finish filing his income tax return.

Other Tax Implications

To fully defer the taxation of a property, the taxpayer must trade for equal or higher value. The value of the replacement property must have value and equity greater or equal to the relinquished property; otherwise, taxation may occur.

Often people want to take cash out from a 1031 exchange or carry a lower mortgage on a replacement property than on a relinquished property. This creates what is called a "boot." The receipt of cash or mortgage boot is taxable to the extent of realizable gains from the sale. The IRS defines boot as anything in a transaction that is not "like kind."

Example:

Henry sells a rental property in a 1031 exchange. The gain on the sale is $250,000. Henry does buy a replacement property, but decides to keep $30,000 to go on vacation. Henry must pay tax on the $30,000 because of the cash boot received.

But let's say Henry has a $50,000 mortgage balance on the property he sold. When the replacement property is purchased, Henry needs to have a mortgage of $50,000 or more, or Henry must pay taxes on the mortgage payoff. In addition Henry is not allowed to take cash boot out and then take a mortgage on the replacement property as an offset. Generally, boot taken can be offset by boot given, but cash boot cannot be offset by mortgage boot given. This is complex, and competent tax advice is essential in implementing this strategy.

5. 1031 Exchanges with TICs

A new type of property ownership is called a tenant in common (TIC). When purchasing a replacement property, the taxpayer buys into an undivided interest in a like kind property. The property is most often a commercial property.

In 2002, the IRS issued Procedure 2002-22, which allows the TIC ownership structure in 1031 tax-deferred exchanges.

Potential advantages from TIC ownership include:

1. *Diversification.* Real estate owners often own property in the same geographic region or own the same property type. Through TIC ownership, clients can own multiple kinds of real estate in different regions. For example, Janet, who owned a highly appreciated duplex in San Francisco, exchanged her property for an undivided TIC ownership of an office building in Indianapolis, a warehouse in Atlanta, and an apartment building in Texas. Janet was able to diversify her investments and spread her risk.

2. *Possible higher returns.* In certain regions in America, property appreciation has increased substantially while rents have lagged. Many TIC sponsor firms use their expertise to locate properties with better rents in different regions. They use their firm's size and experience to negotiate better financing, lease terms, and purchase prices on their replacement properties. This can lead to a potentially higher return than Janet would receive if she acted alone as an individual investor.

3. *Professional management.* The TIC replacement property is managed professionally. This frees Janet from the time-consuming problems of dealing with toilets, trash, and problem tenants. The management company shoulders these functions.

4. *Estate tax planning.* Because Janet owns an undivided interest in a real estate investment, her estate valuation may be discounted. This lower estate value helps reduce her estate tax bill. The valuation discount is based on the TIC ownership (undivided interest). This ownership provides a lack of complete ownership control and liquidity.

TIC ownership can be very appealing, but it is not a solution for all people. Because most TICs are offered as securities, the Securities and Exchange Commission (SEC) has established that only accredited investors can purchase these products. Qualifications are based on net worth, past income, and other factors.

TIC ownership also comes with limitations, including:

1. *Lack of liquidity.* Real estate investments are illiquid compared to stocks, bonds, and mutual funds. With TIC ownership, Janet co-owns these properties with other investors. Properties are generally only sold when a consensus is reached by the co-owners. Most TIC sponsors tell investors that the hold period can be up to 10 years. (Currently, no secondary markets exist for the sale of TIC ownership interests.)

2. *Co-ownership*. As an owner of an undivided interest in a property, Janet co-owns this property with other investors. With this lack of control, the decision-making process is shared. TIC properties can have up to 35 owners. (Who will buy fractional interest in the property?)

3. *Costs and other factors*. Careful review of these TIC offerings and their sponsors is essential. What is the track record and history of the sponsor company? What are the expenses and loads associated with the purchase of this property? It is essential that the taxpayer review closely the prospectus with a trusted advisor, including the underlying financial terms, the assumptions in all projections, the length of tenants' leases, and other considerations that can affect the investment. TIC returns, like other real estate investments, are based on the quality of the property and the financial security of tenants paying rent.

TIC ownership can be an ideal solution for many real estate investors. As always, careful consideration and proper due diligence is essential to successful investment.

6. Other 1031 "Like Kind" Exchanges

One of the essential steps in completing a 1031 exchange is to purchase a replacement property that is "like kind." The IRS has allowed many different types of property to qualify as like kind. Some taxpayers have sold a single-family rental property through a 1031 exchange and purchased replacement property that included apartment buildings, shopping centers, office buildings, raw land, and other real estate.

The IRS looks at the nature or character of the property, not the grade or quality. It has provided additional opportunities that have been beneficial and lucrative for taxpayers over the last several years. Under IRS Revenue Ruling 68-331, a replacement property can include interest in natural resources in the United States.

Some taxpayers exchanged property for real estate that has valuable natural resource interest rights, such as oil and gas or timber. These natural resource rights can be an additional opportunity to provide asset diversification.

Example

A few years back, Mary and Marty completed a 1031 exchange in which their replacement property consisted of valuable oil and natural gas rights. Unlike a working interest in oil and gas properties, royalty owners do not invest in equipment or costs associated with exploration, drilling, or operation of the wells. Large oil and natural gas companies own the wells on these properties. These companies pay the mineral rights holders a royalty based on the amount of oil and natural gas that these wells yield. In most of these programs, a taxpayer holds a small interest in the mineral rights in many different wells in multiple states to help ensure proper diversification.

In the last several years, royalties have been substantial due to increased demand for oil and natural gas worldwide. Cash flow is generally better than with traditional real estate investments. These royalties are not highly correlated with the stock or bond markets. The mineral returns can be a wonderful hedge against rising energy costs. These rights can potentially be sold on a secondary market.

One most always remember that these rights have a useful life. Often, after 20 to 30 years, reserves are depleted.

7. Combining IRC 1031 with IRC 721 for tax deferral and more liquidity

With 1031 exchanges of property, taxpayers can receive the benefits of tax deferral. In many cases, they are still subject to the day-to-day headaches of property management. While TIC properties can end property management headaches, they can offer limited liquidity options and lack of control because of shared ownership. To get the best of both worlds, some taxpayers have been using dual strategies that take advantage of IRC sections 1031 (tax deferral) and 721 (non-recognition of gain or loss on contribution).

How It Works

Assume Tony purchases a replacement property under 1031 to ensure tax deferral. Tony buys an undivided interest through a 1031 TIC investment. At some point in the future, the TIC property will be contributed to a partnership in exchange for operating units—under IRC 721, a nontaxable contribution.

This process is a structural strategy used by a real estate investment trust (REIT). With this strategy, all or substantially all the holdings of the REIT are held inside the partnership, with the REIT being the general partner. The resulting structure is known as an UPREIT (umbrella partnership real estate investment trust). So at the completion of the 721 contribution, Tony owns operating units that carry the economic benefits of the REIT portfolio. Tony receives distributions of operating income and participates in capital appreciation. In the future, he may decide to convert the operating units into REIT shares that can be sold on a publicly traded market. Upon conversion of operating units to REIT shares, a capital taxable event takes place. Shares can be sold to provide immediate liquidity. Tony can manage his conversion of shares over a period of time to take advantage of sound tax planning.

An important consideration in using this structure is that future 1031 exchanges will not be an option available to the taxpayer because the operating units created are not real estate interests.

8. *An Installment Sale*

Many investors prefer the idea of receiving their payments over a period of years and paying capital gains taxes over the same number of years. For clients approaching retirement, an additional source of predictable income sounds ideal.

The Mechanics

- Rudolf negotiates the sales price, including the frequency and amount of payments, with the buyer. For example, a property is sold for $1,000,000. The buyer agrees to pay Rudolf $100,000 now and $100,000 a year for the next nine years.

- Rudolf provides financing for the buyer. The buyer now owns the property with Rudolf receiving a partial payment and a note secured by the property.

- Each year, the seller receives $100,000. The payment is considered in part a return of basis (tax free), part capital gain (subject to capital gains taxes), and part interest payment (ordinary income tax).

Although for many investors the installment sale is great, others are uncomfortable being the bank for someone else. These investors want to feel confident that they will receive their payments as agreed. They want to simplify life and be able to enjoy other pursuits.

9. The Structured Sale (The New and Improved Installment Sale)

For many sellers, the "structured sale" can be the right solution. A structured sale can provide the security that many sellers seek when they are receiving scheduled payments.

The History of the Structured Sale

Over the past several decades, many civil court cases have used an annuity product to fund damages. We often read about a horrific accident in which someone was badly injured. At a civil trial, a jury decides that substantial damages are owed to the injured party. In most cases, these damages require lifetime payments to the injured party. The payments from these lawsuits are often funded by large insurance companies and are called "structured settlement annuities." They provide an annual payment for a period of years or a lifetime. These structured settlements provide the economic assurance that the injured party will receive income in a timely manner.

These large insurance institutions looked at the highly appreciated real estate market and determined their structured settlement product can be used in installment sales...thus, the birth of structured sales.

The Steps to a Structured Sale

- Tia negotiates the terms of the sale of a property with the buyer. For example, with a $1,000,000 sales price, Tia will receive $100,000 now and $100,000 a year for the next nine years.

- The buyer purchases the property and pays cash to an assignment company. The assignment company buys an annuity from the financial institution. The buyer's obligation is transferred to the insurance company issuing the annuity.

- Tia receives the annuity payments over a period of years. The capital gain is recognized and the associated capital gains taxes are paid over those years.

Welcome to the concept of the structured sale. Most of the companies involved are large, well-known life insurance companies. Thus, clients can sleep well at night and feel assured that they will receive each and every payment from the sale of their property.

Comparison with Installment Sale

From Tia's perspective, she receives payments backed by a stable financial institution. Unlike an installment sale, property financing is not provided by the seller. The buyer must arrange for property financing. The "cooperative buyer" of this property can negotiate a better price for the property through a willingness to accommodate Tia's desire to defer and recognize the capital gains tax over a period of years. Under the right circumstances, a structured sale can benefit both the buyer and the seller.

Tia is now able to sell her highly appreciated property without having to pay the tax immediately. She is able to enjoy her payments over a number of years and to pay capital gains taxes over the same time period. Best of all, she is relieved of the worry about the property buyer's ability to pay. The payments are guaranteed by a large financial institution.

IRS Considerations

Many professionals believe the structured sales concept can be an excellent real estate sales planning tool. The large insurance companies have designed these products to best meet the needs of the buyer and seller. Installment sales have existed for many years and have specific rules outlined under IRC section 453. As with any new strategy, the IRS has not yet provided a ruling on structured sales annuities, nor has it commented on them.

10. Charitable Remainder Trusts

While each of the capital gains tax strategies can be beneficial, only the charitable remainder trust (CRT) can eliminate capital gains taxes from the sale of the appreciated property.

The Charitable Remainder Trust

Many investors find a CRT can be a valuable income and estate tax planning tool for selling highly appreciated property. For some taxpayers, using a CRT can help increase their income potential. A CRT can provide lifetime income potential, create a charitable deduction for the taxpayer, eliminate capital gains taxes from the sale of the appreciated property, and eliminate this property from estate tax consideration.

The CRT Steps

- Transfer appreciated property to CRT.
- CRT sells property. Proceeds are invested.
- CRT pays an annual income to taxpayer(s) for their lifetime.
- At taxpayers' death, remaining assets inside trust are transferred to charity.

Additional CRT Features:

1). Income tax deduction: When the appreciated property is transferred to the CRT, an income tax deduction is created. This itemized income tax deduction may help the taxpayer pay less in federal and state incomes taxes. The amount of the income deduction varies with the unique circumstances of each case. The amount is calculated using IRS guidelines which include the value of the property, the age of the taxpayers, payout rates and interest rates established under IRS Code Section 7520. There may be limitations on the amount of charitable deduction an individual taxpayer can take in the current year. If the limit is exceeded, the excess deduction can generally be carried forward up to 5 years.

2) Elimination of capital gains taxes on sale of property: After the appreciated property is transferred to the CRT, the property is sold without capital gains taxes. The proceeds from the sale are invested and designed to provide the taxpayer lifetime income. This means that the CRT is able to invest <u>all</u> the proceeds from the sale with no reduction from capital gains taxes.

3) Provide lifetime income potential: The CRT is required to pay income to the taxpayer (former property owner). There are different types of Charitable Remainder Trusts. The most common trusts utilized with a CRT include a Charitable Remainder Annuity Trust (CRAT) or a Charitable Remainder Unitrust (CRUT). When using a CRAT the annual payment to the former property owner will be a fixed amount each year. With a CRUT the annual payment will be based on a certain percentage (e.g. 6%, 6.5 %, and 7%) of the balance of the trust. The percentage amount will be fixed, but the actual amount received from the CRT will fluctuate with the changing asset

balance in the trust. The amount paid can be monthly, quarterly or annually.

The taxable nature of these annual payments is based on tiered trust accounting. The 4 tiers are ordinary income, capital gains income, tax exempt income, and tax free income. The annual payments will likely be taxed at different tax rates based on the nature of the investment(s) inside the trust.

4) At the death of the taxpayers the income payments cease. The amount remaining in the CRT will be transferred to the taxpayers' designated charity tax-free. These assets are no longer part of the client's estate and are free of estates taxes. Through this generosity, a charitable organization may receive substantial funding. The taxpayer's name can be on a new hospital wing or funding much needed scientific or medical research.

Other CRT considerations

A CRT is not for everyone. A CRT is an irrevocable trust. Once property is transferred to the trust, the taxpayer no longer owns that highly appreciated property. After death the remaining investments in the trust go to charity not heirs.

CRT's with Wealth Replacement Trusts

Many of our clients consider CRT's a good tax and estate planning tool. But often an individual like Tim will comment, "A CRT makes a great deal of sense, but I was planning to leave this property to my children. What can I do to benefit them?"

Our clients often utilize a wealth replacement trust with their CRT. A wealth replacement trust is designed to replace the value of the property given to the charity at the death of the taxpayer. Most people can purchase a life insurance policy on the life of the taxpayer(s) to create value for the heirs. In many cases a client can use a small portion of the income received from the CRT to pay for this insurance. The insurance policy is designed to pay at the death of the taxpayer(s). With proper planning the death benefit is paid to the heirs, income and estate tax free....thus replacing the value of the appreciated property originally transferred to the trust.

With a CRT many parties can benefit including the taxpayer, heirs, charities and the IRS. Yes, even our friends at the IRS. The IRS has long recognized the importance charities play in our society. The federal government directly uses many charities to help achieve national goals in social, scientific and medical endeavors.

Each individual should seek professional advice to determine if a CRT is right for that person's unique circumstances.

The Conclusion

Clients who own highly appreciated real estate have numerous different planning opportunities available. Careful consideration to an individual needs and tax planning are important to insure success in selling highly appreciated property. Good professional guidance is essential.

Chapter 8

College Savings 101

Contributing Author Jennifer Blake Karaczun

This material is not intended to replace the advice of a qualified tax professional. Before making any financial commitment, consult with your tax adviser.

NEXT Financial Group, Inc. does not provide tax advice.

We do our best to help our kids prepare for college. We tell them to eat a healthy breakfast, to turn off the TV, and to do their homework. We hope to provide our children with a quality education that can open the door to a lifetime of fantastic opportunities.

However, are you doing all you should be doing to prepare yourself financially for one of the biggest undertakings your family will likely experience? After planning for retirement, the second biggest concern for most families is funding a college education.

Unlike planning for retirement, your time line for college savings is fairly short. If you get an early start, you may have 18 years. For people who are starting later, it's less time. Planning ahead, preferably soon after your child is born, is the key to success. Systematic savings of even small amounts, when wisely invested over a child's lifetime, can add up to some pretty sizable numbers.

Many people feel the price of a good education for their children is growing beyond their reach and are shocked by the staggering figures they see for the rising costs of education. Although the costs of education continue to rise faster than inflation, we can put it in perspective. The current cost of 4 years tuition at a public in-state college or university is approximately $30,000. According to the National Automobile Dealers Association, the average price of a new car sold in the United States is about $28,400. So, if your family can find a way to budget and plan for a new car every few years, then it's likely that a college education is also within your reach.

How can you make the best investment choices for the education of your children? Many ways to save for college have been around for years, such as UTMA/UGMA accounts and savings bonds. Coverdell ESAs are a more recent introduction, and the new kid on the block is the section 529 plan.

Although every family is different and there is not one simple solution that works for everyone, 529 plans are an attractive solution for many families.

In this chapter, we will discuss how 529 college savings plans work and attempt to alleviate some of the confusion surrounding them. We will also compare them to other methods of funding an education. This will give you a good basis to begin an important conversation with your advisor as to which savings vehicle, or combination of vehicles, is best suited for your family.

Named for section 529 of the Internal Revenue Code (IRC), the 529 plan began in 1997 as a program to encourage families to invest for education expenses by offering them tax advantages. Also known as qualified tuition plans, 529s are sponsored by states, state agencies, or educational institutions. Anyone, regardless of age or income, can open a 529 plan for any beneficiary he or she chooses. These plans can be started with a large lump sum or a small contribution, making them very flexible to fund. Add to this a few unique benefits regarding ownership and control that you won't find in any other savings vehicle and you can see why they have so quickly become popular and attractive investment options for millions of families.

The first major benefit to investing with 529 plans is, of course, the tax advantages. The money you invest grows tax deferred. You don't pay any tax on the growth, interest, or dividends that the account accumulates through the years. We all know that tax deferral can have a dramatic effect on the growth of an investment, particularly a long-term investment. Then, as long as the assets are withdrawn for qualified expenses, the withdrawals are also exempt from federal income tax. The tax-free treatment, which was due to sunset at the end of 2010, has been made permanent with the Pension Protection Act of 2006. This means you can save in a 529 plan and be assured that your withdrawals for qualified education expenses will remain free from federal income tax. This has made 529 plans even more appealing than before.

Since 529 plans are associated with states, many people mistakenly believe this limits either their choice of plan or their choice of college. This is one of the most common sources of confusion. A few plans do have residency requirements, but the vast majority of them do not. With a few exceptions, you do not need to be a resident of a particular state to participate in that state's 529 plan or to be the beneficiary of one. Neither do you have to participate in a particular state's plan to attend college in that state. For example, a grandma who lives in Washington can open a Colorado plan for the benefit of her grandson who lives in Pennsylvania, and who eventually goes to college in Michigan.

Let's take a moment to clarify some of the basics. The person who opens the account and deposits money – either in a lump sum or in installments over time – is the contributor.

The good news is that anyone can contribute to a 529 plan. There are no age restrictions or income restrictions. Anyone, regardless of what they earn or what their age is—parents, grandparents, family, and friends—can establish and contribute to a 529 plan for the benefit of anyone they choose. The person who is intended to use the money, the future student, is the beneficiary. The contributor and the beneficiary don't even have to be related. Each plan can only have one named beneficiary at a time.

It's important to remember that the contributor is the person who will always have all control over the account. This is one of the key advantages of investing in 529 plans. The contributor, based on his or her investment objective, chooses a fund or portfolio available within the program and then makes contributions to the fund according to his or her wishes. The contributor also decides the amount and timing of any withdrawals that are taken. The contributor can change investments or change plans. The contributor can even change the beneficiary. The beneficiary never, ever takes ownership or control of the account. This is reassuring for people who want to ensure that the funds they've earmarked for education are going to be used for that purpose.

This is dramatically different from the rules surrounding a UGMA or UTMA account. This is the common way most people help their children save. Unfortunately, if you open one of these accounts for your child or grandchild, you only have control over these accounts until the child reaches the age or majority. That might be age 18 or 21 in your state. At that time, these accounts automatically become the property of the minor. Upon reaching the age of majority, the child can take the money and do whatever he or she wants with it – buy a sports car, go on a tropical vacation, anything. We all hope our children turn out well, but sadly that isn't always the case. Even if your clear intention was to use the account for your child's education, you child is not obligated to honor your wishes. You have absolutely no say in the matter.

Many people like the control of the 529 plan for just this reason. The contributor decides under what circumstances withdrawals can be taken. The beneficiary never has access to the account.

Many people are pleasantly surprised to find that 529 plans are so easy to start and easy to contribute to. The minimum amount to establish a plan varies, but is often $1,000 or less. Many plans will also allow you to make systematic investments as low as $25 per month, and the maximum amount you may contribute per beneficiary is quite high. The amount varies from plan to plan, but it is often in excess of $300,000. Whether you're starting with a small or large contribution, whether you're planning to invest regularly or with a single lump sum, 529 plans can be flexible, convenient, and accommodating too many different lifestyles. With such flexibility in funding, 529 plans can fit in many budgets.

Currently, every state has at least one 529 plan and there are dozens of choices available. How do you choose? The first place to start is your home state. Many plans will offer special incentives to in-state investors. For example, in New Jersey, several benefits are available to residents (e.g., the annual fee is waived if the contributor or beneficiary is a New Jersey resident, a so-called "scholarship" of up to $1,500 is available toward freshman year at an in-state college or university if you meet a few conditions). A few states will let you deduct some or all of your contributions from your state income taxes if you use the in-state plan. Other benefits that some state plans might offer to residents include matching contributions, exemption from state financial aid calculations, reduced annual fees, or protection from creditors. For some people, these can be very compelling reasons for choosing an in-state plan.

Of course, you shouldn't stop there. Your state's plan is not necessarily the most suitable one for you. Many important factors can influence your choice. A bit of research might lead you to discover that an out-of-state 529 plan may offer other benefits. Perhaps you're interested in a different investment selection, a more attractive selection of investment features, lower expenses, a money manager whose investment philosophy is most aligned with your future goals, or other feature that is appropriate to your specific needs.

Certainly, one of the primary factors to consider when selecting a section 529 plan is the plan's performance history. However, 529 plans are all quite new, so it can be very difficult to interpret any kind of track record on such a short performance history. In addition, every state program has different portfolios with different investment options, making it difficult to make apple-to-apple comparisons.

Of course, investment in a 529 plan does not come with any guarantees. It doesn't guarantee that your savings will be enough to fully cover tuition and expenses. It doesn't guarantee that your child will go to college or be accepted by any particular college. It's just a way to help concerned families accumulate the money they anticipate they'll need for future tuition. As with any investment, the account earnings will be a based on a combination of how much you've contributed, how long you've been invested, and how the investments performed over that time.

That's why it's critical to discuss all these concerns with your advisor. Together, you can determine the best plan for your unique circumstances.

As previously discussed, the main advantage to investing in 529 plans is the tax advantage. Assets withdrawn from 529 plans are free from federal income taxes as long as they're used for qualified education expenses. Qualified expenses include tuition at accredited schools and institutions. This means it can be used for undergraduate or graduate studies at your local community or junior college, a state college, a private college, or a university. It can also be used at many trade, professional, and technical schools within the U.S., as well as hundreds of colleges and universities abroad.

Don't forget that UGMA and UTMA accounts are going to be taxable to the minor. All the interest, dividends, and capital gains each year from the UGMA or UTMA are reported under the child's social security number. This is what we commonly called the "kiddie tax." Therefore, the tax deferral feature of the 529 plan is very valuable.

However, some people prefer the flexibility of savings or investments in UGMA/UTMA accounts since these accounts can be used for any purpose at all, as long as the benefit is to the minor child. Certainly you can use the accounts for college, but often people have other savings goals for their children in addition to education, such as helping them save for a car, a house down payment, a wedding, or starting a business. UGMA/UTMA accounts carry the maximum flexibility for withdrawing for any reason.

Beyond tuition, there are many other expenses associated with a good education. Other qualified expenses at your college may include room and board, fees, books, and required supplies and equipment. You can also use the assets in your 529 plan for all these qualified expenses.

Although the 529 assets will grow tax deferred, be aware that the contributions will not be deductible on your federal tax return. Some states, however, may offer a state tax break, such as a tax deduction for your contributions or an exemption on withdrawals. Although earnings are exempt from federal income tax, they may be subject to state income tax.

One frequent question is, "What if my child doesn't go to college?" Today, most people need some kind of secondary education to have a successful career. Most people just can't excel in life with only a high school diploma. Their career path may not take them along the university route, but it could include trade school, part-time college, or some form of professional training. Regardless of when and where your child gets an education, as long as the education comes from an accredited institution that is eligible to participate in U.S. Department of Education student aid programs, you can use 529 plan assets.

Some children might decide at age 18 that they aren't ready for college. Fortunately, the assets can wait. Another important feature of 529 plans is that there are generally no time limits on the life of the account. In most plans, funds need not be used by a certain date; instead, the account can remain open for as long as there is a named beneficiary. You can leave the contributions invested for a later time. After all, your child may decide at age 25 or 35 or 55 to further his or her career, and then he or she will have the opportunity and the financial ability to do so.

What happens to your 529 plan if your child gets a full scholarship to college and doesn't need the money? (Lucky you!) Well, you can use the 529 plan assets to cover expenses that the scholarship may not cover, such as books and fees. Another point to keep in mind is that upon graduation with an associate's or bachelor's degree, many bright scholarship-worthy students will be planning to further their education with graduate school or various continuing education programs. The 529 plan can be used for a masters or doctoral degree also. Again, there is no age limitation, so the assets will be available whenever you decide you need them. Or, you may choose to allow your scholarship student to withdraw the funds. You will not pay a penalty on any amount withdrawn to the extent of the scholarship, although earnings will become taxable to the beneficiary at his or her tax level. The good news is that the tax impact will likely be a negligible amount, assuming the child is a full-time student and not yet in the work force.

If, after all of that, it still turns out that you just aren't going to use the 529 savings for the education of the child for whom it was intended, there are some flexible options. Another unique feature of 529 plans is that the contributor has the ability to change the beneficiary. As long as the new beneficiary is a member of the immediate family, there are no tax consequences for doing so. Fortunately for us, the IRS has very broadly defined the word "family." So, if the student you named as beneficiary doesn't want the money, doesn't need it, or just doesn't use it, you can name a sibling, a niece or nephew, stepchild, aunt, uncle, cousin, or even a parent to be the next beneficiary. The ability to change beneficiaries combined with no time limit is a fantastic combination of benefits that are unique to 529 plans. Think about the impact this could have on future generations! If there are no time limits on the life of the account, and because the donor can change beneficiaries to other family members, the account can theoretically stay open for generations.

Finally, a worst-case scenario, if you choose to liquidate the college savings plan and not use it for qualified expenses, all is not lost. You can take back your contributions. However, any earnings would be subject to state and federal tax, plus there would be a 10 percent federal tax penalty imposed on the earnings, and there could possibly be a state tax and/or penalty.

It's hard to see into the future, so the choices we make today need to be flexible. After all, family circumstances can change, investment climates can change, new opportunities come along, and the original investment choices you made years ago may no longer be the best ones going forward. Many factors can give you reason to reevaluate your original investment. Fortunately, you do get a bit of flexibility with 529 plans. The IRS permits you to change investment options in your 529 account one time in each calendar year, and you will not incur any tax or penalty for doing so. Many people may decide, for example, to move to a more conservative portfolio to reduce market volatility as their child is approaching college. You also might decide that you no longer like the plan you started and want to change to another state plan with a different money manager. The IRS will allow you to completely change plans once a year if you so choose. You can also change options whenever you change the beneficiary designation on that account, but don't forget that any portfolio changes that are made automatically, such as under an age-based allocation option or investment averaging option, are not counted for this purpose.

What about those good old-fashioned EE savings bonds; are they a good way to save for college? In many cases, no. Although they do accumulate interest on a tax-deferred basis and offer some security, they are not as attractive as an investment as they were in years past. Savings bonds have recently lowered interest rates, lengthened minimum holding periods, and added more restrictions. Although savings bonds can sometimes be cashed in tax free for qualified higher education expenses, the rules are quite cumbersome.

First, eligible expenses in this case are defined as just tuition and fees. It excludes the cost of room and board, as well as books and other related expenses. The next problem is that the amount of eligible expenses is reduced by the amount that a student receives as scholarships, fellowships, and other types of tuition reduction. That means the amount of bond interest you can exclude may be decreased. Third, the ability to take a full deduction for interest earned on an education savings bond is only available to bond owners with modified adjusted gross income under certain limits. Finally, to qualify for the tax benefit, the bonds cannot be registered in the child's name. If used for education, and the student is under 24 years old, the bonds must be registered in the parents' names. As a result, many bonds whose purchase was intended for a college education will not be eligible for the tax advantages that the purchaser was hoping for.

Another popular method for saving for college is the Coverdell education savings account (ESA). These plans were originally known as education IRAs (individual retirement accounts). Unlike 529 plans, assets in Coverdell ESAs can be used to pay for qualified elementary and high school expenses as well as college expenses. Families with children in grades K-12 can use the accounts to pay for expenses such as private or religious school tuition, books, uniforms, and supplies.

Coverdell ESAs are available through a variety of mutual funds with long track records, which makes planning and allocation much easier. Plus, investment allocation can be changed at any time, not with the once-a-year limitations on 529 plans.

The primary problem is the low contribution limit. You can only contribute $2,000 per beneficiary per year, or penalties will be imposed. If other family members open accounts and make contributions for this same beneficiary, even if you are not aware of it, there could be problems. Due to the low contribution limit, it is unlikely that most people will be able to save adequate funds for a child's future education. Another concern is that there are strict income limitations on who can open a Coverdell and how much they can contribute. Only individuals with adjusted gross income under $95,000 ($190,000 if married) can make the maximum allowable contribution. A third concern is that the assets in the account must be fully withdrawn by the time the beneficiary is age 30, unless transferred to another beneficiary. Any amount not used for qualified education expenses will subject to a 10 percent penalty plus income tax liability to the beneficiary. Coverdells can be a way for some families who are under the income limitations to provide additional funds for education, but due to their low contribution limits they are unlikely to be able to fund a significant part of your child's tuition.

When it comes to balancing the concerns about saving for college while simultaneously saving for retirement, many parents should consider making contributions to an IRA or a Roth IRA to the maximum amount they are eligible to contribute. Individuals can contribute up to $4,000 per year (or $8,000 per married couple) to either a traditional or a Roth IRA.

Amounts contributed to either a traditional or Roth IRA accumulate on a tax-deferred basis. Although primarily intended as a retirement savings vehicle, distributions prior to age 59½ are not subject to the 10 percent premature distribution penalty if they are used to pay for qualified higher education expenses for the IRA owner, the owner's spouse, child, or grandchild. Note that for Roth IRA owners, to qualify for this tax benefit, the accounts must also have been held for at least five years.

Of course, the IRA owner retains control of the retirement account; the intended beneficiary has no access to the funds and no control over the funds. IRAs can be invested in a wide array of investment choices and, therefore, are more flexible than 529 plans in portfolio allocation and planning.

One drawback to using traditional and Roth IRAs to pay for college expenses is that they have low annual contribution limits. You can contribute only $4,000 each year (or $8,000 if married). As with Coverdells, the low contribution limits make it unlikely you will reach your college education savings goals. In addition, many higher income individuals are not eligible to contribute to Roth IRAs.

Of course, the biggest and most obvious concern is that any amount withdrawn for college expenses won't be there for your retirement! However, for those people trying to balance the dual concerns of saving for college while saving for retirement, this can be an effective tool when used in addition to other retirement and college funding methods.

Although many employers allow you to tap into your 401(k) for college expenses, this is probably not the best plan. Any amount borrowed must be repaid in short order and with interest. If you should leave your job, the loan is most likely going to be called and the full amount will become due.

Prepaid tuition plans are a variation of college savings plans and are also available under section 529. A few states offer prepaid tuition plans under section 529 that allow buyers to purchase semesters of tuition for certain eligible institutions or in-state public schools. Private universities can offer these plans as well. These kinds of 529 plans are pretty much what they sound like: You pay today for a number of tuition credits at today's prices and that amount of credits is guaranteed for the future, regardless of tuition increases, as long as you attend that specific school. Basically, prepaid tuition plans lock in college costs so that tuition inflation doesn't outpace the growth of your savings. Most of these plans are not offered on a national basis, although a few are open to nonresidents.

These types of prepaid 529 plans work best for students who know they will be attending a particular institution. Should your student choose to go to college elsewhere, it may be possible to convert the benefits for another institution, but you should completely understand the conversion formula before making the commitment to join the plan. If your children go to a different school, be prepared to pay the difference. In addition, most prepaid state tuition plans cannot be used for room, board, and supplies, so you will still need to save separately for that.

How does all this saving impact the ability to get financial aid? First, many families are surprised to discover that college aid isn't "free money"; it mostly consists of loans. Current studies estimate that up to 59 percent of financial aid is in the form of loans. It's not all grants, scholarships, and work-study programs. As a result, many students are graduating today with a crushing amount of debt. Whatever savings you can accumulate for college expenses may help reduce both the parents' and the student's future debt load. Given the choice, most parents would rather plan ahead and be prepared to pay with their savings rather than burden their child with unnecessary and overwhelming amounts of debt.

You should also understand that most financial aid is need based. It's based on a mathematical formula, taking into account the student's income and assets and the parent's income and assets. This is weighed with some other factors, such as family size, age of parents, and number of children in college. All of these numbers are considered and "crunched," and the final figure is called the EFC, or expected family contribution. This is how much the government expects your family to contribute toward education. The lower your EFC, the more aid you are eligible to receive.

Bear in mind that a significant part of the formula is based on your household income, but it doesn't take into account your lifestyle choices like credit card debt and car loans. It would be wise to reduce your non-essential debts and increase your monthly cash flow well before your child applies for college.

Any asset that is owned by a student or the parent of a student can potentially affect aid. Generally speaking, the more you save, the less your need is. While savings may decrease financial aid, you will most certainly be in a much better financial situation if you save for college. After all, the more you save, the less you will need to borrow. It doesn't make any sense to avoid saving for college with the hope of receiving financial aid. However, when it comes to making smart choices about saving for college, there are a few places that are more strategic to save than others.

Retirement accounts generally do not count as assets available for education costs. This includes IRAs, Roth IRAs, 401(k)s, and annuities. As long as retirement accounts don't count as an asset, it makes sense to have fully funded your retirement accounts before funding other areas that could be counted as assets available for education. For this reason, it doesn't make sense to overfund your child's college fund to the detriment of your own retirement security. However, if you should take distributions from your retirement account toward education for your children, the distribution is counted as income and may slightly decrease your next years' aid.

A section 529 plan owned by a parent has minimal impact on financial aid. As with other assets of the parents, including bank accounts, brokerage accounts, and mutual funds, about 5.6 percent of the value of the asset is considered in determining the EFC. The same goes for Coverdell plans. However, distributions made from a 529 plan are resources that reduce need on a dollar-for-dollar basis the next year.

In addition, payments from a prepaid tuition plan are considered a family college resource, so any distributions will reduce financial need on a dollar-for-dollar basis.

For financial aid planning, the worst place to save money is in the child's name, such as in a UGMA or UTMA. Assets that are in the name of the student are valued at 35 percent in determining the EFC. If you have saved significant amounts of money by this method, it may be advisable to make a large purchase before applying for aid. If your child needs a car or computer for college, this may be the time to buy it.

For concerned grandparents, 529 plans can offer some fantastic estate planning solutions. For seniors who are interested in removing assets from their estate but not willing to give up control, 529 plans provide a very attractive solution. Upon making a gift of a 529 account, the value is removed from your taxable estate. However, as previously discussed, the beneficiary never takes control of the account. You, as the contributor, decide if and when any distributions are taken. In addition, a unique feature of 529 plans allows you to revoke your gift and take the funds back for yourself for any reason, although tax and penalties may apply. Other types of gifts (e.g., UGMA/UTMA) are not revocable, ever, under any circumstances. Many seniors are intrigued by this idea of removing assets from their estate but still maintaining full control over them.

Generally speaking, a person can contribute up to $12,000 annually ($24,000 for married couples) to another person, such as a grandchild, without triggering a gift tax. Another unique feature of 529 plans is the ability to accelerate your wealth transfer by investing up to $60,000 ($120,000 per couple) per beneficiary in a single year and spread the gift tax exclusion over five years. Of course, you can't make any other gifts to this beneficiary during the same time period and should you pass away within the five years, a prorated amount of the contribution may be included in the taxable estate. UGMA/UTMAs are ineligible for this benefit and Coverdells are, of course, limited to $2,000 per year and are thus also ineligible.

Although it can be a great tool in estate planning, accelerated gifting can create problems for Medicaid eligibility. The problem is that the revocability of a 529 plan makes it a countable asset in determining Medicaid eligibility. Each contribution you make is countable for Medicaid determination for 60 months. Of course, eligibility for Medicaid may not be your goal. Many seniors would be better served by strategic planning and purchasing a long-term care policy rather than trying to reduce their assets to poverty level.

Your tax advisor together, with your attorney and financial advisor, can help you navigate this rather tricky but valuable opportunity and ensure that you understand all the rules and limitations.

Don't overlook one more great way to use a 529 plan - for yourself! You can open your own account, name yourself as beneficiary, and take advantage of the tax benefits. For any adult who plans to further his or her education at a later date, this is a fantastic opportunity. Planning to go back to college or get your MA in a few years? Open your own 529 plan. Young and active retirees – take note! Have you always dreamed about going back to finish that degree? Want to study a foreign language, or take an art history class, tennis lessons, or computer classes after retirement? Consider funding your own 529 plan and fulfill your retirement dreams. After finishing your education, you can name a child or grandchild as the beneficiary of any amount you don't need to use for yourself. Not only would you provide an outstanding example of the value of an education to the younger generation, you can provide a funding legacy as well.

Section 529 plans can offer a fantastic opportunity for many families to help build savings for future college needs, but no solution is right for everyone. As you have seen, there are many college savings choices. Be sure to consider the specific needs of your family, and take into account your budget, your time horizon, your risk tolerance, your concerns for flexibility, control, tax advantages, and other considerations. Your advisor will help you compare and understand the different options and help you determine what course of action is right for you.

With a few smart choices today, plus a little creative planning and a bit of discipline, you can make a significant impact on the future of the children you love. You can give them the everlasting gift of a good education, and lay the foundation for a bright future.

Chapter 9

Women, Wealth, and Worth
Why a Chapter Just for Women?

Contributing Author Julie Gneiser

"Women, if you are given a choice between money and sex appeal, take the money. Believe me, as you get older, the money will become your sex appeal."

Katherine Hepburn said those words long before it was fashionable for a woman to be savvy about money and investing. Always blunt, she was apparently very wise, as well! She must have known, then, that times were changing, and women's roles would be drastically affected. What worked for our female ancestors is now, truly, ancient history. Never before has it been more important to become financially independent. It is the perfect time for a woman to take control of her own future. No longer should she depend on someone else, even the government, to ensure her security.

As women crush barriers in political arenas, career settings, and family dynamics, they continue to grapple with their "feelings." Traditional responsibilities and roles, such as caring for children or aging parents, can feel as if they are derailing career goals or sabotaging opportunities. This is further compounded by a rising divorce rate and the fact that, if married, it is not only conceivable, but likely, that a woman will outlive her husband. However, the very good news is that never before has a woman had so many choices in how she wants to live her life. Robin McGraw states in her new book,

Inside My Heart, "The real privilege is being free to embrace the joyful aspects of your life and reject the hurtful ones, to choose what is working and to turn your back on what isn't. It's a privilege and a right to take charge of your existence and be excited about your life." Simply put, the rules for women have been relaxed and the options expanded. Today's female is entitled, even has the moral responsibility, to choose how she wants to live her life as a woman!

It is true that a woman can be handed circumstances throughout her life that are not of her choosing, and these circumstances can create some overwhelming obstacles. Today, however, a woman must understand what she can and cannot control, and accept that what she does...or leaves undone...contributes to her distress or her success. Along with the privilege of defining who she is and how she wishes to live comes the acknowledgment that she is fully responsible for her choices.

This chapter is intended to inspire women to make an investment of time and education to develop financial strategies. In her book, *Rich Women*, Kim Kyosoki says that only 20 percent of baby boomer women will be secure in their retirement years. This means that 80 percent will not be financially secure! Not to worry; ever since the cavemen days, women have been resourceful and proactive. Today, they are planners and they are emotionally invested in their long-term goals. More importantly, women are creative problem solvers and more assertive than ever before. I believe, with the exceptional developmental opportunities and an existing culture that is encouraging them to become more independent, women will make the commitment to "learn to earn" and the 80 percent figure will drop, sooner rather than later.

Many strong women, who have added value to many other lives, can lose all confidence when it comes to financial concepts. This insecurity is perpetuated by a lack of knowledge and a dependence on others, including spouses, accountants, lawyers, and even financial advisors. A woman with this disposition takes her first step to achieving financial security and independence by speaking with an advisor. The next step requires her to choose to equip herself with knowledge. By taking the time to study or attend seminars, she continues her journey to attain financial clarity. This will eventually bring her peace of mind about her financial destiny. A woman must empower herself to participate in decisions that will ultimately affect her own life and the lives of her loved ones.

Women's incomes are rising. Over the last three decades, nearly all income growth has been on women's side. Since 1970, women's median income has increased a whopping 60 percent, while men's barely rose 1 percent! Also, women now represent half of stock market investors and control nearly half of the estates in this country valued at more than $5 million! Furthermore, one of the fastest growing sectors of this society is that of female-owned businesses, which generate more than $3.6 trillion in annual revenues. These statistics, provided by the 2006 study, "Women, Power, and Money," by Allianz Life Insurance Company of North America, are truly optimistic.

This is all great news, and certainly about time! So what's the problem? It is apparent that America is a great place for a motivated and passionate woman to thrive. What, then, are these special issues and needs that are suddenly attracting so much attention, as evidenced by the rash of recent books, television shows, and seminars?

Women Might Need an Attitude Adjustment

While maintaining enormous family responsibilities, many women also have strong aspirations to elevate themselves in a professional or personal area of their lives. They set high standards for spending adequate time as mother, wife, daughter, sister, and friend. This softer side of the female psyche just won't go away...thank goodness! Women are also notorious for battling guilt. They continue to be primary caretakers for their own children and aging parents. They tend to put other people first, often with disastrous results when it comes to financial planning. As nurturers, women can sometimes fool themselves into believing that if they just do the right thing for others, things will work out for the best.

In her book, *The Secret*, Rhonda Byrne writes that thoughts of wealth and abundance are necessary for individuals to obtain the things in life that they most wish for. The premise here is that an individual must generate positive feelings, and visualize his or her desires. This adjustment in the mind should adjust the actions, and eventually the universe will respond and what will flow into an individual's life will match those positive feelings. This book and DVD have taken the country by storm and the book has remained on the best sellers list for 10 months. Are Americans, especially baby boomer women, grasping for a tender-hearted way to acquire wealth and prestige? Everyone agrees, one cannot find happiness without a positive attitude and a life based on making wise and ethical choices. I doubt that the intent of this book, or those by any of the other well-respected authors on fulfillment and success, is written to encourage individuals to live their lives void of responsibility and hard work. Surely, successful people must establish long-term and short-term goals and a road map to follow to achieve them. Then, they need a motive to remain enthusiastic. Could one motive really be money?

A woman takes in many messages from her private world that shape her attitudes about money and power. How she processes those messages has more to do with years of conditioning as she grew up than what she really wants. It is not superficial to want wealth. To be ambitious about this goal does not have to mean a woman will lose who she is. To intend on being rich does not imply arrogance, but rather necessary goal setting. Money plays a bigger role in women' lives than they would like to admit. The bottom line for any woman is that without money, the ability to follow her dreams, for self and loved ones, is seriously impeded, regardless of how ethical or worthy those dreams are. The lack of money can actually make her feel as if money runs her life. However, fortunately, it is possible to set financial goals using your heart and your head.

Women and Men Have Different Financial Needs

The purchase price of a vehicle or the interest rate on a mortgage is the same for men as it is for women. Goods and services cost the same regardless of gender. The principles used to achieve good investment results are the same for everyone. So, what are the real differences between men and women when it comes to investing? Why is the financial industry finally sitting up and taking notice of women? It is because men and women are not the same when it comes to money matters.

Women definitely have different financial needs than men. This is the direct result of their female perspective and startling labor and mortality statistics. Even with the enormous changes occurring in the work force, the fact remains that women still earn less than men. The Bureau of Labor Statistics, 2007, reports that a woman is paid 74 percent of what a man with similar education and experience is paid. This demonstrates just how far behind the female gender has been in terms of compensation!

Longevity is also a major concern for women. All couples want to believe that they will grow old together, but for the vast majority it just is not so. Today's retired women are expected to live 10 years longer than retired men. Baby boomer women (born between 1946 and 1964) are estimated to outlive their husbands by 15 years or more. The average age of widowhood today is 56 years old. Yes, three-fourths of women are single when they pass away. Ninety-five percent of women in the U.S. will have sole responsibility for their finances, yet most have not figured out a financial plan. These statistics are provided by Women's Institute for a Secure Retirement, *What You Need To Know – Your Future PayCheck*. Sobering information, it suggests that baby boomer women might have to stay in the work force well beyond 70 years of age, if they have not accumulated enough retirement assets or if they continue to need group health insurance coverage. Longer life spans, combined with the reduction of social security benefits and increasing medical costs, are compelling reasons for any woman to put together a financial plan.

Another intimidating issue for women revolves around the alarming, and well-known, fact that half of marriages in this country end in divorce. Although divorce affects both husbands and wives, it appears that women suffer the greater losses. One might argue that wives and mothers get alimony, child support, and maintenance, not to mention some of the husband's retirement fund if hers is smaller than his. Anyone reading this probably knows women who are financially secure and living well after a divorce. On the other hand, with women's income levels rising, divorce decrees will likely reflect this, and alimony will likely decrease.

However, as it stands today, the painful truth is that within the first year of a divorce, a woman's standard of living in this country drops an average of 43 percent, according to a study done by Women's Legal and Defense Fund, 2005. To add insult to injury, the income of the non-custodial parent (still typically the man) generally rises after a divorce, writes David Bach, bestselling author of *Smart Women Finish Rich*.

Even though two-thirds of the female population is currently in the work force, and over half of all household income is earned by women, there is a dilemma. This most overlooked issue for working women is the effect that time spent out of the work force has on their potential to build wealth to secure a comfortable retirement. Responsibilities of child rearing and caring for elderly parents causes women to move in and out of the work force more often than men. Women spend more than 14.7 years out of work. For every year that a woman stays home to care for an aging parent or to provide child care, she must work five years to recover lost income, pension coverage, and career promotions. Women who take an average of eight years caring for aging parents lose an average of $659,139 in lifetime wages, pension, and social security benefits. These are not top executives, but women earning an average of $35,000 a year. These figures result in less money saved for retirement, according to the National Center for Retirement Statistics, 2006.

Statistics can only tell the probability of a situation occurring. A woman cannot know, in advance, if she will become divorced or widowed, or find herself having to care for an ill child or parent. Then there is the possibility of becoming disabled herself. If she is single and passes away, who will help take care of her children? Special challenges require special solutions. These situations can devastate perfectly normal lives, and knowing her options ahead of time, can make a drastic difference in the outcome for a woman or her family. Taking control of her finances and building a plan for the future can allay many fears.

Women Need to Define Themselves

What does this mean for a woman? It means that she must be proactive. The previously stated financial and personal realities confront a woman every single day. Consequently, this calls for some tenacity and common sense in choosing which battles to fight. She must figure out how to remain balanced while taking care of herself and so many others. *A woman cannot afford to become too busy to take the time to assess her values and her current situation.* What is really the most important thing to her? It is probably not money itself, but she shouldn't kid herself. Having money grants a woman the freedom to choose, with purpose and integrity, what kind of woman she wants to be. Without money, there are fewer choices, and she can become a victim her of circumstances.

However, a woman can set herself up to win, no matter what happens. Information and education are the best remedies for financial concerns. Procrastination and passivity are a woman's worst enemies. She needs to invest in herself and do some serious soul searching about what is important in her life, what she really wants in the long run. However uncomfortable or awkward she feels, she must just plow ahead! With her true values in her mind and concerns about money spelled out on a tablet, it is time to connect with a financial advisor and devise her new strategic financial life plan or to "tweak" her existing plan to match those values.

Be Willing to Learn

Learning about wealth building and how to become a financially independent woman is more than just a practical matter. Women can develop their financial skills, and learn the nuts and bolts of financial planning. The other part of the process is the emotional shift that has to take place for many women. If a woman resists taking action, even though she knows the steps she needs to take, it may be time to reexamine her own fears. Barbara. Stanny repeats in her book, *Prince Charming Isn't Coming,* that it is "self-deception" to ignore the hard-nosed fact that we have to take care of ourselves. Sure, for some women, reading financial literature and managing their investments is not a big deal. However, many women still feel vulnerable and would rather work on more traditional areas of personal development. Why do you think women's magazines still concentrate on fashion, weight loss, cooking, gardening, traveling, and child rearing, devoting only an average of about 3 percent to finance? Women prefer those subjects! The learning curve for understanding finances seldom gets discussed.

There are wonderful books written for women, including the great sources cited at the end of this chapter. Joining an investment club, or even starting one up, is a fun, and not-too-risky, way to learn while getting some hands-on experience in personal investing and evaluating investment ideas. Most seminars that are geared for women are worthwhile. Whatever a woman does to learn something new, increase her financial vocabulary, or gain a new perspective regarding money will contribute to her confidence now, and her success later.

Men and Women Want Different Things from Their Advisor

From the onset, women view their financial advisor differently than men do. Truthfully, a woman is usually more risk averse than a man. This causes her to be cautious and diligent in her homework. This might cause her to procrastinate or do nothing at all. But women are proactive. Not afraid to get help, a woman will ask many questions and is more likely to work with a professional. A man is usually more interested in the advisor's history of returns, training, fees, and similar information. A woman will pick an advisor based on feelings of trust and honesty. A woman generally wants someone who will educate her before she discusses any financial goals. She will look for someone who tries to understand her current situation, feelings, and personal goals.

Remember that building wealth is more than an interest or a hobby for a financial professional; it is a full-time job. If a woman has chosen an advisor who understands her, then that advisor should be able to assist her in planning her financial future at every stage of her life. Planning for each stage of life is an ongoing process and requires revisiting the plan every so often as life changes. This is the only way to ensure that her plan is attainable and coincides with her priorities. She must periodically reassess and identify what she values most at this point in her life, and this will define what she needs to focus on to achieve her personal goals and wants.

Women Make Great Investors

Investors cannot expect upside potential of the market without accepting downside risk. There is no advisor's crystal ball, and while actively buying and selling investments in the short term may appear to be "getting a jump on the market," one simply cannot win in the long term. *The one thing that makes women potentially better investors than men is their ability to commit to the long term.* This is one place where a woman's cautious disposition may work in her favor. Reacting slowly, a woman investor sticks with her financial strategy, one that was predetermined by her and her advisor. This requires discipline, but because she trusts her advisor, and together, they have devised a plan, she is comfortable. She is less likely to react to market swings, which can result in trailing the market.

Any investor can get caught up in investing on a hot tip, instead of investing in what is making money. Men can be more restless, always shopping for a deal, absent of the advice of a professional. Believing that their stock pick is going to come back, they often hold on too long and end up selling at a loss. It is ironic that men, who are criticized for being emotionally detached in other area of their lives, may be less able to detach from the emotion of investing. Women are currently better investors, reaping higher returns in the stock market than their male counterparts, as reported by countless articles. Of course, successful investing is about the individual, not the gender. It is about knowledge, discipline, and experience. The statistics only prove that women can, and should, be investing. This contradicts that lack of confidence about investing that seems to prevail among otherwise confident women!

Invest, Invest, Invest

Investing entails risk…and sometimes volatility. That's the way it is. But the biggest risk a woman can take is to do nothing. Experiencing those waves of regret does not have to happen. Barbara Stanny, daughter of Richard Block of H&R Block, and the author of *Secrets of Six Figure Women*, had the unfortunate experience of a first marriage that left her in debt and devastated emotionally. She has since rebuilt her life and become famous for her coaching programs that help women build wealth. Ms. Stanny has this to say: "This is not rocket science. To protect our future and ensure our peace of mind, we must take an active role in creating our own wealth." A woman needs to understand that it is paramount to be prepared for whatever life may throw at her.

As devoted caregivers to others for most of their lifetimes, many women have no plan in place to care for themselves in a life-changing emergency, or even in retirement. It is not enough to work hard and maintain a frugal lifestyle, women must invest. And they must do so wisely. Staying invested and managing those investments is a priority during both pre- and post-retirement years.

Unless a woman is planning to retire within 24 months, she should be invested for growth in her retirement accounts. Women invest their pension assets too conservatively, according to the American Council of Life Insurance Study, 2005. Realizing that she might live longer than a man, she has to make her money last longer! Women sometimes make the mistake of playing it safe with their retirement accounts, and that is a grave mistake. Remember that this is a long-term investment. Growth investing means stocks and mutual funds that invest in stocks. To accumulate enough assets to comfortably retire, the money a woman invests must be working as hard as she is. Once these assets have been accumulated, women must also establish financial strategies that will protect and preserve these assets during long retirement periods, so they don't outlive their money

Consolidating Assets Makes Sense

Recently I met with a 57-year-old woman. She was contemplating retiring within five years and wanted me to review her current situation. After a brutal and costly divorce in her mid-forties, this woman had structured a divorce decree that assigned her husband responsibility to pay for her college education instead of splitting his individual retirement account (IRA). A forward-thinking woman, she worked her way up the corporate ladder and had socked enough away to begin to consider retirement. As expected, there were two old 401(k) accounts and her current one. There was also an IRA, a small stock portfolio, and one large mutual fund. These investments were held by several brokerage firms, multiple advisors, and a bank. In our discussion, it became apparent that this woman worked hard and was a saver, and she believed that she must invest, thus explaining the abundance of accounts. She also declared herself a balanced investor when it came to risk. She had attended various company 401(k) providers' seminars and understood the importance of being diversified. She was set…now she just needed to know if she had enough investments to retire in five years.

This woman was proud of how she had battled her way to the top in a little over a dozen years. She had accumulated significant assets only because she was determined and she had kept on course through several tough spots in her life. She deserved a lot of credit and, therefore, I proceeded carefully so as not to diminish these true accomplishments.

Common Diversification Misconceptions

The following example shows how investors can misunderstand the term *diversify*.

My client was confused about the meaning of diversification. Diversification refers to spreading moneys over several asset classes, such as different types of stocks, mutual funds, and bonds. This is the best way to reduce volatility and minimize risk. When I took inventory of her various accounts, she had no bonds and the same large cap growth fund in all three of her 401(k) accounts and in her IRA. She also held a risky amount of international funds. Finally, her stock account had barely grown in four years. Essentially, she had overlap and gaps in her overall portfolio. Knowing she had several accounts, and within each account she had various funds, she believed she was diversified as a whole.

She could have completely diversified her investments by consolidating her accounts into one IRA custodial account. Within that one IRA, and with one advisor being able to see all of her assets, she could do a better job of controlling how she is diversified. When assets are held in many different accounts with many advisors, it may be impossible to do achieve investment goals!

Rebalancing Is Important

The same example can illustrate why the process of rebalancing is important: My client was beginning to feel a bit frustrated. She acknowledged that she might have too many accounts, but, nonetheless, she had set those accounts up to be balanced. She wanted to know why she had so much in international growth, as she clearly remembers telling those advisors and the 401(k) custodians that she tolerated only moderate risk!

Setting up an account is not a "set it and forget it" proposition. It requires some adjustments. In our example, over time, the international growth assets had stronger returns than her other asset classes. This caused a shift in how her portfolio was divided. Eventually, her portfolio was not allocated at all like a balanced investor's; she was actually looking more like she was aggressive. Occasionally, even in a well-diversified portfolio, all investors need to rebalance their assets. Rebalancing will ensure that her money is invested according to her goals and will also maintain her desired portfolio allocation.

Roll Over That 401(k)

Leaving a company retirement plan behind can mean big trouble later. My client was lucky. If one of her former companies had changed 401(k) plans, there is a good chance that her assets could have been frozen for a time and she would not have been able to reposition them. Had the company not been able contact her, it would have had to transfer the money into the new plan. Because the company cannot allocate the money for her, the money would probably have been placed in low-earning money market funds.

The worst-case scenario with multiple 401(k) accounts happens when the account owner dies. Her beneficiaries, who are her adult children, would have to go back to both companies and provide death certificates, verify that she was an employee and her dates of employment, and submit the necessary identification to prove they were her named beneficiaries. This is cumbersome and can take up to a year to process.

Together we determined a strategy that would allow my client to retire in no more than five years. She rolled over the two 401(k) accounts and the old IRA into one consolidated IRA, with a more balanced asset allocation model that matched her time frame. She would visit with me again in six months, at which time we would review the account and probably rebalance. She decided to sell her stock, at a loss (therefore fewer taxes), and establish an emergency savings account. We took $5,500 of the mutual fund and established a Roth IRA, which she will continue to fund each year via the mutual fund. And finally, she committed to max funding her current 401(k) for the next three to five years.

Mortgage Strategies

Women, in general, detest having big bills. If a women receives a large sum of money, usually from an inheritance or a life insurance policy, her first impulse is to hurry and pay off her mortgage. Assuming she will be better off by paying the biggest bill she has, it feels like this is the best choice. This may not be the most prudent decision. Some women might be better off keeping the mortgage and investing that money elsewhere. If invested wisely with a decent return, and there is no guarantee it would be, she could use it to supplement her income or retirement assets. This scenario makes sense if her mortgage is currently at a reasonable interest rate, and she has built up some decent equity.

Many mortgages were refinanced in the last few years when interest rates reached 40-year lows. Although this reduced investors' premium payments, in many cases they increased their debt as they rolled credit card debts, vehicle loans, and other bills into their new mortgages. A woman who finds herself in this situation should start making extra principal payments. She should call her lender and find out how much extra she needs to add to her monthly premium to pay off the mortgage earlier. She should always make sure the bank applies the extra to the principal At these low interest rates, paying extra principal can substantially shorten the time until she owns her home.

Estate Planning Is Essential

A woman who spends a lifetime taking her responsibilities as a wife, mother, or daughter very seriously, and then dies without an up-to-date will or living trust is being irresponsible. That sounds harsh, but by neglecting to prepare estate planning documents, a woman is basically giving Uncle Sam permission to decide how to divide her estate. As well, there is nothing set up to minimize the estate taxes or attorney's fees her heirs will have to pay. This is minor compared to the stress on the family of a seriously ill or disabled woman, if she has not designated a power of attorney for health or finance.

Remember that women control nearly half the estates over $5 million? Why do you think that is? Frequently, it is because they have outlived their spouses and now are responsible for handling the entire family legacy that was built while they both were alive; now all the decisions surrounding the estate fall to her. Even though money and other prized possessions or real estate are not the most important part of the legacy one leaves behind, how assets are divided among the heirs can create an emotionally charged family discussion and make life miserable for any mother. Estate planning issues should be resolved long before estate issues arise! An attorney who specializes in estate planning and will work cooperatively with your trusted financial advisor can assist in formulating this planning.

Women Have to Make a Choice

This chapter has outlined only a few general strategies for successful investing. It is inappropriate to give any type of specific advice unless there is an established relationship and a woman reveals her current situation, feelings, and goals. Every woman should make sure she is with an advisor who listens to her and questions her about her values and fears. She needs to feel that her advisor is someone she can trust.

If a woman is part of a couple, then meeting with an advisor should probably be a joint effort. Having each party handling specific tasks is not a bad idea as long as both parties are in the loop. It is important to encourage questions and to expect answers. Launching into financial discussions is not a "fun" exercise, and very often people put it off until it is conveniently forgotten. It takes emotional discipline to have this discussion, and it can be easier if a coach is at the table (e.g., the trusted family advisor).

In almost all relationships, there are times when partners do not agree about what is important. A woman will consider others' feelings when wanting to make changes. She may hesitate to contact an advisor if her partner is reluctant or uninterested. But, she has the choice to move forward on her own and ask her partner to respect her decision, even if the partner chooses not to participate. Or, a woman can do nothing, and this is also a choice. Either way, each woman is responsible for her own choices.

The Process Is Worth the Work

This chapter refers to assets, and makes some recommendations for helping those assets prosper and thrive. A woman's most precious assets are not material. They are intangible but necessary for true inner peace. Her character and her values will motivate her to act with integrity as and after she attains her financial goals.

Every new skill or shift in thinking requires practice. Who a woman becomes in the process of achieving financial independence is more important than the financial independence itself. The past is not important, the only important thing is where a woman wants to go with her life. Following the law of attraction, if a woman wants to discover who she is, she must take a close look at her relationships and her activities. This calls for honesty and courage.

It is never too late to become the person you were meant to be. Even as late as her 50s and 60s, a woman has opportunities to put her life on the right track, says David Bach in *Start Late, Finish Rich*. She must become a "do it now" person, and defeat procrastination as it relates to making changes in the areas of her life that matter most to her. There is no limit to the learning opportunities that are before her. To obtain financial success, she must commit to doing what it takes to get smart about money.

The end goal is not to become a highly trained and educated financial professional. True wisdom is not formal education. A woman must seek both wisdom and knowledge in her life. The goal is to become an activist in her own life. Knowledge leads to confidence and power. Wisdom arrives when a woman develops awareness and learns from her mistakes. She becomes wise and knowledgeable, which generates confidence. Confidence will inspire action. Wealth building starts when she begins to make her own prudent decisions. True abundance happens when she appreciates her assets, tangible and intangible.

Money does a woman no good if she does not know how to use it. The measure of a woman is how she uses her wisdom and her resources to define her life. How she shares what she has learned, how she touches others — this is what will alter her from within. No matter how much money a women acquires, the ultimate satisfaction is seeing it managed according to who she is and what she stands for. The choice is hers.

Chapter 10

Qualified Plans for Business Owners

Contributing Author David Parker

If you are a business owner who has employees, then you are going to want to offer a retirement plan. Retirement plans allow your employees to save for the future. They can direct a portion of their income into these plans, and they put off paying taxes on that income until they retire. Most of the plans require or allow an employer to contribute to employees' retirement. The plan you choose will affect your net income, the amount of taxes you will have to pay, and the amount of future obligations that you will have to pay out. Therefore, it is important to make sure you choose the plan that is best for your business. This chapter describes the different types of retirement plans available.

Simplified Employee Pension (SEP)

A SEP is a form of profit sharing, having a contribution limit of the lesser of 100 percent of compensation or $42,000. The major advantage of this form of plan is reduced documentation and reporting requirements.

In exchange for simplicity, it requires very early eligibility for employees and equal treatment for all those covered.

Ideal Investor

A small firm seeking to minimize filings and paperwork is the ideal investor. One short form sets it up and investments are made to an IRA. It may exclude employees with less than three years of service during the previous five years and those under 21.

Plan Contribution Features and Limits

Contributions are limited to the lesser of 100 percent of earned income or $45,000 for each individual.

Special features include:

- Easy to establish
- No government filings
- Extended deadline for plan setup
- Full flexibility of contributions
- 100% normally vested immediately

Salary Reduction (SARSEP)

A salary reduction simplified employee pension plan (SARSEP) is a SEP plan set up before 1997 that permits contributions to be made through employee salary reductions, referred to as "employee elective deferrals." Under a SARSEP, employees and employers make contributions to traditional individual retirement accounts (IRAs) set up for the employees, subject to certain percentage-of-pay and dollar limits.

Employees can play an active role in funding their retirement by choosing to have the employer contribute part of their pay to their separate IRAs, referred to as SEP-IRAs. SEP-IRAs need to be established for each participant, even those becoming eligible after December 31, 1996, with a bank, insurance company, or other qualified financial institution.

New SARSEPs cannot be established after December 31, 1996. However, employers who established SARSEPs prior to January 1, 1997, can continue to maintain them and new employees hired after December 31, 1996, can participate in the employer's existing SARSEP.

Ideal Investor

A business with 25 or fewer employees wanting to offer employees a way to invest through convenient salary reduction in before-tax dollars is the ideal investor. This plan limits contributions by the business. It has a special non-discrimination test, and it may exclude employees with less than three years of service during the previous five years and those under 21.

Plan Contribution Features and Limits

There is a salary reduction arrangement up to the lesser of $15,500 for 2007. Regulations may require a business contribution in top-heavy plans. New SARSEPs cannot be created.

Catch-up contributions are allowed for those older than age 50.

Special features include:

- Simple, inexpensive 401(k)
- IRA replacement
- Promotes employee participation
- 100% normally vested immediately
- Special non-discrimination test
- No new SARSEPs allowed

SIMPLE IRA

The SIMPLE (Savings Incentive Match Plan for Employees) IRA is a simplified, tax-favored retirement plan for small employers that provides for elective contributions by employees and meets certain vesting, participation, and administrative requirements. This plan permits contributions only under a qualified salary reduction arrangement. A qualified salary reduction arrangement is defined as a written arrangement of an "eligible employer" under which:

1. Employees eligible to participate may elect to receive payments in cash or contribute them to the SIMPLE IRA.

2. The amount to which such an election applies must be expressed as a percentage, or dollar amount, of compensation and may not exceed $10,500 per year (2007).

3. The employer must also make matching contributions or non-elective contributions to the account.

4. No other contributions may be made to the account.

In 2007, the maximum elective deferral amount is $10,500 and the maximum catch-up contribution is $2,500.

An individual who defers $10,000 to a SIMPLE IRA of one employer and participates in a 401(k) plan of another employer would be limited to an elective deferral of $5,500 in 2007 ($15,500 - $10,000) to the 401(k) plan.

The requirements for the employer's matching contributions or non-elective contributions are discussed below.

Matching Formula

Under the matching formula, the employer is generally required to match employee elective contributions dollar for dollar up to an amount not exceeding 3 percent of the employee's compensation. However, a special rule permits the employer to elect a lower percentage matching contribution for all eligible employees (not less than 1 percent of each employee's compensation). To get the lower percentage, the employer must notify employees of the election within a reasonable time before the 60-day period for electing to participate in the plan.

The employer may not use the lower percentage if the election would result in the percentage being lower than 3 percent in more than two of the five years ending with the current year. If the employer (or a predecessor employer) has maintained the plan for less than five years, the employer will be treated as if the percentage were 3 percent in the earlier years during which the arrangement was not in effect. If the employer made non-elective contributions for a year (instead of matching contributions) under the formula described below, it would be treated as having 3 percent in that year.

The compensation limit under IRC section 401(a)(17) does not apply for purposes of the matching formula; therefore, the 3 percent match could reach the maximum of $10,500 (2007) for an employee with compensation of $350,000 in one year.

A matching contribution made under this provision on behalf of a self-employed individual is not treated as an elective employer contribution for purposes of the limit on such contributions. The purpose of this provision is to treat self-employed individuals in the same manner as employees with respect to the limit on elective contributions.

Non-Elective Contribution Formula

Instead of matching contributions, an employer can elect to make a non-elective contribution of 2 percent of compensation on behalf of each eligible employee with at least $5,000 in compensation from the employer for the year.

If the employer makes this election, it must notify employees within a reasonable time before the 60-day period for electing to participate in the plan. The compensation limit under section 401(a)(17) applies for purposes of this formula. Thus, the maximum amount that could be contributed in non-elective contributions for an employee would be $4,500 (i.e., 2 percent of $225,000 in 2007).

An arrangement will not be treated as a qualified salary reduction arrangement if the employer or a predecessor employer maintained another qualified plan (including a 403(a) annuity, a 403(b) tax-sheltered annuity, a SEP, or a governmental plan other than a section 457 plan) under which contributions were made or benefits accrued for service during any year in which the SIMPLE IRA plan was in effect.

However, if only employees other than those covered under a collectively bargained agreement are eligible to participate in the SIMPLE IRA plan, this rule will be applied without regard to a collectively bargained plan. In addition, for purposes of this rule, transfers, rollovers, or forfeitures are disregarded except to the extent that forfeitures replace otherwise required contributions.

Eligible Employer

Only an eligible employer may adopt a SIMPLE IRA plan. An "eligible employer" is defined as an employer that employed no more than 100 employees earning at least $5,000 from the employer during the preceding year.

For purposes of this limitation, all employees employed at any time during the calendar year are taken into account, even those who are excludable or ineligible to participate. Furthermore, certain self-employed individuals who receive earned income from the employer during the year must be counted for purposes of the 100-employee limitation. An employer that maintains a plan in which only collectively bargained employees may participate is not precluded from offering a SIMPLE IRA to its non-collectively bargained employees.

Generally, an eligible employer that ceases to be eligible after having established and maintained a SIMPLE IRA plan for at least one year will, nonetheless, continue to be treated as eligible for the following two years. However, special rules apply where a failure to remain eligible (or to meet any other requirement of section 408(p)) was due to an acquisition, disposition, or similar transaction involving another eligible employer.

Contributions under a SIMPLE IRA plan may be made only to a SIMPLE IRA, and a SIMPLE IRA may receive only the defined contributions and rollovers or transfers from another SIMPLE IRA. All contributions to a SIMPLE IRA must be fully vested and cannot be subject to any prohibition on withdrawals or conditioned on their retention in the account. However, the premature distribution penalty for withdrawals is increased to 25 percent during the first two years of participation.

Participation Requirements

The participation requirements for SIMPLE IRAs state that all non-excludable employees who received at least $5,000 in compensation from the employer during any two preceding years, and are reasonably expected to receive at least $5,000 in compensation during the year, must be eligible to make the cash or deferred election (if the matching formula is used) or to receive non-elective contributions (if the non-elective formula is used).

Of course, employers are free to impose less restrictive eligibility requirements, such as a $3,000 compensation threshold, but they may not impose requirements that are more restrictive. The $5,000 threshold compensation amount is not scheduled to be indexed for inflation. Nonresident aliens who received no U.S. income and employees subject to a collective bargaining agreement generally are excludable employees for purposes of the participation requirement. An employee who participates in another plan of a different employer may participate in a SIMPLE IRA plan, but will be subject to the aggregate limit of $15,000 (in 2006) on the exclusion for elective deferrals. An employer that establishes a SIMPLE IRA plan is not responsible for monitoring compliance with this limitation.

Tax-exempt employers and governmental entities are permitted to maintain SIMPLE IRA plans. Excludable contributions may be made to the SIMPLE IRA of employees of tax-exempt employers and governmental entities on the same basis as contributions may be made to employees of other eligible employers. Related employers (i.e., controlled groups, partnerships or sole proprietorships under common control, and affiliated service groups) must be treated as a single employer for purposes of the SIMPLE IRA rules, and leased employees will be treated as employed by the employer. Consequently, all employees (and leased employees) of an employer who satisfy the eligibility requirements must be permitted to participate in the SIMPLE IRA of a related employer.

A SIMPLE IRA is not subject to non-discrimination or top-heavy rules, and the reporting requirements it must meet are simplified. A SIMPLE IRA plan must be maintained on a calendar-year basis.

Compensation, for purposes of most of the SIMPLE IRA provisions, includes wages (as defined for income tax withholding purposes), elective contributions made under a SIMPLE IRA plan, and elective deferrals, including compensation deferred under a section 457 plan. A self-employed individual who is treated as an employee may be a participant in a SIMPLE IRA plan; for this purpose, "compensation" means net earnings from self-employment, prior to subtracting the SIMPLE IRA plan contribution. An employee's elective deferrals under a 401(k) plan, a SARSEP, and a 403(b) annuity contract are also included in the meaning of compensation for purposes of the 100-employee limitation (i.e., the $5,000 threshold) and the eligibility requirements.

Administrative Requirements

The administrative requirements for SIMPLE IRA plans state that an employer must make elective employer contributions within 30 days after the last day of the month with respect to which the contributions are to be made, and that matching and non-elective contributions must be made no later than the filing date for the return for the taxable year (including extensions).

Employee Right to Terminate

Employees must have the right to terminate participation at any time during the year; however, the plan may preclude the employee from resuming participation thereafter until the beginning of the next year. A plan may (but is not required to) permit an individual to make other changes to his or her salary reduction election during the year (e.g., reducing the contribution amount).

Generally, each employee must have 60 days before the first day of any year (and 60 days before the first day the employee is eligible to participate) to elect whether to participate in the plan, or to modify his or her deferral amount.

Special features include:

- It is a smaller and simpler version of a 401(k).

Keogh or HR-10 Plans

Self-employed proprietors or partners may establish a tax-sheltered retirement plan under the provision of HR-10, the Keogh Act. The result is a tax deferment of the top dollars earned, plus a shelter of all earnings on these deposits until retirement.

The fund can grow substantially by the "magic" of compound interest and the interest on dollars that would have been paid in taxes during the accumulation years. The maximum contribution is the lesser of 100 percent of current earned income or $44,000 (for 2006 as amended by EGTRRA and subject to indexing for inflation in future years).

For purposes of the deduction limit, earned income of a self-employed individual does not include the contribution on behalf of the self-employed person. In determining his or her adjusted gross income, a self-employed person deducts plan contributions directly from gross income – the deduction is allowable whether or not he or she itemizes deductions.

Execution of a Keogh plan requires guidance by a financial planner since you can inadvertently fall into several traps. There are several options.

Defined Contribution

Option 1 - The contribution formula you initially establish locks you in at that percentage. In other words, no flexibility exists. The formula might be a fixed percentage of all employees' wages, such as 10 percent.

Option 2 - Each year you determine what percentage of wages you want to contribute, retaining total flexibility. This is referred to as a profit sharing type of Keogh plan.

The combination of both options provides for flexible planning. For example, under Option 1, 5 percent could be committed, and then under Option 2, a percentage may be determined not exceeding the maximums for defined contribution plans.

Defined Benefit Pension

Option 3 - A plan may also be established that will allow larger contributions, based on funding a specific retirement benefit. If there were only a few years until retirement, this would produce a very large payment, which may be desirable for some individuals. This type of plan calls for a large fixed contribution and is normally suitable for older owners.

Investing Pension Proceeds

Funding may occur through a variety of investment vehicles, including bank accounts, money market funds, annuities, mutual funds, real estate, and bonds. There are advantages to each.

The situation, time until retirement, and other investment holdings will dictate the most effective funding method.

Receiving the Benefits

Funds may be withdrawn in a lump sum and taxes paid on the entire amount (special 10-year averaging rules are available if you were age 50 on or before January 1, 1986). A series of payments, such as an annuity guaranteed for life, can also be taken.

A tax penalty of 10 percent is required for withdrawals made by plan participants prior to age 59½ (unless disabled); withdrawals used for higher education expenses, up to $10,000 for a first-time home purchase, or self-employed health care expenditures are allowed. (change OK and correct?)

Keogh funds are includable in the gross estate for federal estate tax purposes. Also, the funds may be paid to a non-marital trust to escape taxation at the death of the surviving spouse.

Accumulated funds may also be converted to an annuity, using a variety of the funding products offered by life insurance companies.

Reporting Requirements

In 1982, the Tax Equity and Fiscal Responsibility Act (TEFRA) was signed into law. The effect on Keogh plans is described in the following paragraphs.

On or before July 31, 1985, individuals who have established Keogh plans must have filed IRS Form 5500-C. Form 5500-C covers investments, income, and expenses from the previous year and is five pages long, with questions related to plan administrators, funding arrangements, and vesting.

Form 5500-C must be filed in the first year of reporting and every third year thereafter.

Form 5500-R, a two-page form, can be filed in intervening years, or Form 5500-C can be filed for each and every year.

Failure to file could result in Internal Revenue Service (IRS) penalties of $25 per day per Keogh account, up to a maximum of $15,000 unless reasonable cause is established.

For taxpayers on a calendar-year basis, IRS extension Form 5558 must be filed on or before July 31 of the current reporting year for a two and one-half month extension. For taxpayers on a fiscal year, the deadline is the last day of the seventh month following the end of their fiscal year.

Profit Sharing Plan

A profit sharing plan is normally considered by a young company with a history of fluctuating profits. Due to uncertain future earnings, the amount the owner would be willing to contribute is relatively small. However, if the company has a particularly good year, it would like the ability to make a larger contribution.

Also, consider the age of the owner and employees. If they are young (40s), it is another indicator for profit sharing. The reason is that a profit sharing plan is a form of defined contribution plan, which favors younger employees due to the greater number of years for making contributions, time for investments to produce significant yield, and, in this case, the allocation of forfeitures to long-term employees.

Look for turnover and tenure. Even an older owner may benefit from a profit sharing plan if turnover is high since he or she will normally receive the greatest portion of nonvested forfeitures.

Ideal Investor

A firm where cash flow and income are somewhat variable is the ideal investor. This is ideal for a firm wanting flexible contribution levels from year to year. It may exclude employees under age 21 and those with less than two years of service.

Plan contribution features and limits include:
It allows the lesser of 100 percent of earned income or $45,000 for each individual. Contributions may vary based on profits. The thrift plan version permits employee contributions. Employer deduction limit is 25 percent of employee compensation.

Catch-up contributions are allowed for those over age 50.

Special features include:
- It features full flexibility of contributions.
- Part-time employees may be excluded.
- A vesting schedule may be used.
- It requires full reporting.
- Integration is available.
- Employee contribution is permitted.

Money Purchase Pension

A money purchase pension plan is a type of defined contribution plan. That is, the actuary or plan administrator determines (usually by formula based on gross or net profit) the contributions that will be made on behalf of the participants. This is the only plan discussed here that has required contributions. Once the plan contribution is set, that amount must be contributed each year and an excise tax applies if the minimum contribution is not satisfied.

The maximum contribution is similar to most defined contribution plans, the lesser of the participant's compensation or $42,000 (in 2005) per participant. A money purchase plan is not precluded by another retirement plan.

The owner usually is fairly young or is trying to benefit young key employees, such as younger siblings or children, in the firm.

This plan holds appeal when profits have been stable and/or growing and show a promising future. The contribution commitment is higher than with a profit sharing plan.

Ideal Investor

A firm with substantial income is the ideal investor. This is ideal for a firm wanting to maximize contributions at a fixed percentage. It may exclude employees under age 21 and those with less than two years of service.

Plan Contribution Features and Limits

The limit is the lesser of 100 percent of earned income or $45,000. Annual contributions are generally required once installed.

Special features include:
- It maximizes deductible contributions.
- Part-time employees may be excluded.
- Vesting schedule may be used.
- There is full reporting.
- Integration is available.

401(k) Plan

A 401(k) plan is a type of profit sharing plan. The employer can choose to match the employee savings in this plan. This provision acts like a "sweetener" or extra benefit for rank-and-file employees. The important feature is that the employee's contributions are treated as adjustments from gross earnings rather than a deduction, as with an IRA. Even though it is subject to the overall contribution limitation, most employee/employer contributions will not be that high.

Consider the 401(k) when an employer must provide an additional benefit due to possible union involvement or when there are no funds to provide additional benefit packages.

This plan is also suitable when the employer may not be able to commit to a large contribution, but employees are extremely interested in contributing on the most tax-favorable basis. Furthermore, if the employer has a year of high earnings, additional contributions may be made.

Ideal Investor

The ideal investor is the larger firm where the majority of employees defer a portion of their salary. It is ideal for businesses desiring to contribute on a match basis. There are special non-discrimination tests for deferrals. It may exclude employees under 21 and those with less than one year of service.

Plan Contribution Features and Benefits

- There is a $15,500 (for 2007) cap on elective deferrals.
- Catch-up contributions are allowed for those age 50 and older.

Special features include:

- Consulting and plan design

- Comprehensive recordkeeping
- Competitive fees
- Employee communications package
- Vesting schedule that may be used for the employer contribution

Defined Benefit Plan with a Flat Benefit Formula

There are two areas to review with this type of plan. The first is the plan itself, while the second is a type of formula.

A defined benefit plan is one in which an actuary determines the benefits each participant will receive at retirement. Using those figures, it is simply a matter of determining funding (payments) needed to arrive at future values. Therefore, the benefit is known but the contribution is not. Each year, the actuary recalculates the contribution since the assumptions are rarely going to be exact. Interest earnings, or losses, will have a great effect on annual plan costs.

This type of plan is frequently used when dealing with an older owner who is looking to shelter a large sum of money. In the case of a defined benefit plan, the highest annual benefit payable under the plan (or under all such plans aggregated, if the employer has more than one) must not exceed the lesser of (1) 100 percent of the participant's average compensation in his or her highest three consecutive years of employment while an active participant or (2) $170,000 (in 2005 as indexed). Depending on the age of the owner, it could take substantial sums, especially for older individuals since there may not be much time to fund the plan. The defined benefit plan is an ideal plan for older ages, because it offers the ability to make a large financial commitment. It is suitable for companies with stable profits and taxable income.

A flat benefit formula deals only with salary, that is, when the actuary is determining the benefit, only salary is taken into consideration.

For example, a flat benefit pension formula may state that the participant will be eligible for 50 percent of compensation. Therefore, if compensation were $50,000, the participant would be eligible for a retirement benefit of $25,000 per year. A larger portion of the contribution is given to the owner under these conditions. Quite often, the owner will be seeking maximum contributions since he or she is usually making a substantial income and retirement is near.

Defined Benefit Plan with a Unit Benefit Formula

The facts stated above hold true under the unit benefit formula except for the way retirement benefits are determined. Under the unit benefit formula, compensation and years of service are taken into consideration.

For example, the formula may state that each participant will receive 2 percent of salary for each year employed. Therefore, Mr. A, who makes $50,000, would be eligible for $1,000 times the number of years he has been under the plan. If he had been employed for 40 years, the benefit would be $40,000 per year at retirement.

Frequently, the owner or key person of a small to medium-sized business will have worked for the organization since he or she was quite young and consequently accumulated a substantial number of years of service. He or she may also have valued employees who also contributed much of their lives to the organization. Under these circumstances, the unit benefit formula may be the answer.

Look at the personnel profile sheet. Check to see how long the owner and key employees have worked in relation to the rank and file. If there is a difference great enough to justify greater benefits to those the owner would like to reward, use the unit benefit formula.

Plan Contribution Features and Limits

Costs are normally borne by the employer, but some plans require the employee to make nondeductible contributions, generally as a percentage of compensation.

Section 457 Deferred Compensation

Plans of deferred compensation described in IRC section 457 are available for certain state and local governments and non-governmental entities tax exempt under IRC 501. They can be either eligible plans under IRC 457(b) or ineligible plans under IRC 457(f). Plans eligible under 457(b) allow employees of sponsoring organizations to defer income taxation on retirement savings into future years. Ineligible plans may trigger different tax treatment under IRC 457(f).

Ideal Investor

This plan is installed and administered by the government agency, which can limit choices.

Plan Features and Contributions

Employees may contribute up to 100 percent of earned income, subject to a maximum of $15,500 (for 2007).

Special features include:

- It covers the administration of payroll adjustments.
- Contributions to a 457(b) plan are tax deferred.
- Earnings on the retirement money are tax deferred.
- It allows individual enrollment and investments by the employee.

Common Qualified Plans

These are the key features of the most popular qualified plans. Some firms use a combination to derive maximum benefit.

	Profit Sharing	Money Purchase	401(k) Plans	Defined Benefit
Admin. costs	Low	Low	Relatively high	Relatively high
Employer contribution	Discretionary	Required contribution	None required	Required, actuarially determined
Amount that can be contributed	Maximum is 25% of covered payroll	Maximum is 25% of covered payroll	No minimum; discretionary matching	Maximum and minimum vary according to benefit established and investment results
Employee contribution	None	None	Up to $15,500 in 2007	None
Suitability of this type of plan	Companies that want maximum flexibility	Consistently profitable companies	Most companies	Companies that want to benefit older and/or highly compensated

	SEP	SARSEP
Admin. costs	Low	Low
Employer contribution	Varies based on plan	None required
Amount that can be con-tributed	Lesser of 25% of covered payroll or $45,000 in 2007 ($46,000 in 2008)	Lesser of 25% of covered payroll or $45,000 (in 2007; $46,000 in 2008)
Employee contribution	None; employer contributions only	Up to $15,500 in 2007, or $20,500 if over age 50
Suitability of this type of plan	Small business with variable earnings	Small business of 25 or fewer employees; plan must have started before 2007

	Sec 457(b)	SIMPLE IRA	Keogh
Admin. costs	Low	Low	Moderate
Employer contribution	Discretionary	Required contribution	Required
Amount that can be contributed	Up to $15,500	Either matching employees contribution dollar for dollar up to 3% of pay, or 2% contribution for each eligible employee	Up to $44,000
Employee contribution	Up to $15,500	Up to $10,500 in 2007, or $13,000 if over age 50	None
Suitability of this type of plan	State and local government or nonprofit organization	Small business with fewer than 100 employees	Self-employed or partners

Sources: Financial Planning Consultants, Inc.

TMI Tax Services, Inc.

Tax Facts 2007, National Underwriter Company

Tax Facts 2006, National Underwriter Company

Tax Facts 2003, National Underwriter Company

http://www.irs.gov/retirement/article/0,,id=117337,00.html –SARSEP

http://www.irs.gov/retirement/article/0,,id=108940,00.html – SEP

http://www.irs.gov/retirement/article/0,,id=108941,00.html – SIMPLE IRA

http://www.irs.gov/retirement/article/0,,id=172430,00.html - 403(b)

http://www.irs.gov/taxtopics/tc451.html - IRA

http://www.irs.gov/retirement/article/0,,id=137307,00.html - Roth IRA

http://www.irs.gov/retirement/article/0,,id=172437,00.html – 457(b)

Chapter 11

Planning Your Retirement

Contributing Author Anthony Untersee CFP

Welcome to retirement! If you are near, at, or beginning the retirement phase of life, congratulations! There are, however, several areas of your financial future that may require review to maintain or enhance your fiscal fitness. Now is a good time to review your budget, investment and income planning, insurance coverage, and estate planning.

Your income and expenses will likely have significant changes. While you may spend more or less, your discretionary expenses (travel, hobbies, recreation) may increase, while some of your fixed expenses may decrease (mortgage, transportation).

What are your income sources? Traditionally, people were able to rely on a company pension, social security, and their personal savings to fund retirement. Today, though, fewer people are covered by pensions as more companies have transferred that responsibility to employees. Life expectancies are increasing, and so it becomes of paramount importance to evaluate the lifestyle your personal savings can support.

The portfolio of a 45-year-old in accumulation will likely look very different from that of a 65-year-old who is beginning distribution. How reliable is your income, what percentage is derived from a variable source (i.e., stock market), and what is a sustainable withdrawal rate given your expected portfolio return?

It may be helpful to think of sequencing pockets of money (e.g., cash reserve, income producing, and rest-of-your-life money). Using appropriate financial products and tools may help to maximize the efficiency of your resources and minimize taxes and the risk of running out of money.

Ultimately, your needs and objectives, risk tolerance, and time frames for these moneys will help dictate the allocation of your assets. Additionally, taxes, inflation, and the rate of return needed to overcome these must be considered when structuring or restructuring your investments.

You may also want to review your insurance coverages. If you are under 65, health insurance costs may have been partially employer paid and could now be substantially higher. If you are 65 or older, carefully review the various Medicare supplement plans and their providers.

Consider long-term care insurance. Medicare does not cover custodial care and, with costs that can easily exceed $40k to $50k per year, this could represent a serious weakness in your financial plan. Would your spouse be impoverished due to income/asset spend down, or would your legacy for your children be at risk?

Also, evaluate your life insurance. Do you still need the coverages that were necessary earlier in life? Will your spouse need income, do you want to leave a legacy, or do you have potential estate tax liability?

Finally, if you have an estate plan, review it and your beneficiary designations on IRAs, annuities, and life insurance to ensure that beneficiary designations are relevant and up-to-date. If you don't have a plan, hire a qualified estate planning attorney to create one. Typically, powers of attorney for property, health care (if you become incapacitated), and a medical directive are included and part of a basic plan.

The current estate tax law is set to expire in 2010, and it is unknown what the applicable exemption amount will be going forward. If you have potential estate tax liability, life insurance (see above) can be an effective way to provide liquidity to your estate. While life insurance is income tax free, it is not estate tax free so it might be important to have this asset owned outside your estate. Often this is done by creating an irrevocable life insurance trust (ILIT) to own the policy.

While all of this evaluating may seem daunting, it is really a matter of taking a good look at your financial circumstance and using financial tools, techniques, and strategies to maximize your resources to achieve your goals.

You may want to consider hiring a qualified financial advisor to create a comprehensive, integrated financial plan to assist your planning and help provide you with peace of mind.

Chapter 12

Planning for Healthcare in Retirement

Contributing Author Richard Horner

Health care and its related costs must be properly planned for in order for a well-deserved, lengthy retirement to be enjoyed to its fullest. One of the first things pre-retirees ask when planning for retirement is how much health insurance will cost when they leave their job. They are shocked when they find out. Premiums, benefits, and networks vary widely from region to region—even county to county. The average premium for a 60-year-old in California can be as much as three times the amount for someone in Indiana.

Each person must ask the following questions: How am I planning to protect myself from financial catastrophes caused by health care costs, including insurance premiums, prescription medications, and unforeseen health care expenses due to an accident or sickness? If an unfortunate accident causes me to need extensive therapy or I am diagnosed with a disabling illness like Lou Gehrig's disease, Alzheimer's, or diabetes, how will I pay, and where will the money come from? How will these expenses affect the rest of my retirement plans, recreation, and income?

This chapter discusses a major crisis that many retirees face, factors that contribute to the problem, and solutions that, with the help of a trusted financial advisor, can be implemented to plan for your future. Said simply, the crisis is that many retirees are not prepared for the real cost of retirement, particularly in health care expenses. Some of the causes are obvious, such as constant inflation and a longer life expectancy, which translate into savings stretched over a longer period of time. This chapter also introduces options for coverage and provides guidelines for choosing what best suits your needs.

If you have never had to pay for your own health insurance, one piece of advice is be prepared to be somewhat overwhelmed, and that's before you even see the premiums. The common reaction to health insurance premiums for those 55 to 64 is astonishment. Most people have no idea how high the premiums can be. For individuals with existing health conditions, using several prescription medications, or who do not meet ideal height and weight requirements, premiums can be even higher. Individual health insurance premiums may often seem out of reach even for those who have accumulated comfortable amounts of assets during their working years.

Background: Reasons for the High Costs

The major reason health care expenses can catch a retiree off guard is inflation. We all know that everything goes up in price over the years. So does the cost of health care, a healthy lifestyle, and insurance premiums. Health care is rising faster than the cost of living and is not expected to slow down. As a person ages, he or she tends to use health care more frequently and finds expenses never planned for, and diseases and maladies never anticipated. Inflation and future health go hand in hand as frightening partners no one can avoid.

Not only does the retiree need to take into consideration the rise in heath-related expenses over time, but the retiree also needs to understand the varying costs for care associated with different locations. Where a retiree lives can determine both the cost and quality of care. Higher quality care will ultimately cost less, because a procedure done correctly the first time will be less of a financial burden than a procedure done incorrectly and redone. In many retirement communities, especially those located near the coasts, the costs of professional medical services tend to be higher and the quality of locally available medical services and related professionals tends to be much lower. In contrast, younger and potentially more skilled doctors are being attracted to states in the upper Midwest, where compensation is higher and better quality can be expected. For example, Minnesota is the highest rated state for health care with the best success rates for the care delivered. Highly recognizable clinics like the Mayo Clinic, whose reputation in known the world over, are located in Minnesota.

Another factor in growing health care expenses is lengthened life expectancy. Today's Americans can expect to live well beyond their parents. The additional years have been gained by better living conditions and medical science. With more people living longer, the problem of increased morbidity arises. People are living longer, but the final years require more medical treatment and a lot more money. The harsh reality is that people are living longer than they or anyone ever thought was reasonably possible. Today's retirees are expected to live in retirement potentially longer than they ever worked. This, in a worst-case scenario, can mean living longer than they are financially prepared for, and outliving their savings. For past generations, this was never the expectation as they entered the work force. Many began working in their teens and continued working until their 50s or 60s. Their average age of death was 60 to 62 years, prior to ever receiving one dime from social security.

Perhaps the most unfortunate reason health care expenses often exceed retirees' budgets is that employees can no longer rely on businesses to keep promises made decades ago regarding pension and health care benefits. Employers have moved the responsibility of providing health care funding from the business to the individual.

Another area of concern for retirees is the total loss of health care benefits as more and more companies disappear into bankruptcy. Unlike pensions, which are backed by the Pension Benefit Guaranty Corporation (PGBC) and provide promised benefits to affected workers and retirees, there is no such protection when it comes to health care benefits. Health care benefits are not guaranteed, nor are they protected.

Fidelity Study

So just how much money does an individual need to be adequately prepared for health care costs in retirement? Many people have already seen headlines such as:

The Average Cost of Health Care in Retirement for 2007 Is $215,000

This amount is taken from the update of the annual Fidelity Investments study on average costs for health care for couples retiring at age 65 and living for approximately another 20 years. The study has shown that health care may be the single largest expense in retirement, eclipsing travel, recreation, and housing expenses. Many people who plan for retirement believe that they will retire debt free and that most of their income and assets in retirement will be used to pay for basic items like food, shelter, utilities, grandchildren's wants and needs, and recreation. The Fidelity study demonstrates that health care is possibly the biggest overlooked item when planning for the retirement years.

To achieve a better understanding of the numbers, a closer look needs to be taken at how they were derived.

(See next page)

Types of Expenses Cost	Annual Cost	Monthly Cost
Medicare A Premium	$ 0	$ 0
Medicare A Deductible	$ 231	$ 19
Medicare A Co-Pay	$ 51	$ 4
Medicare A Skilled Care	$ 77	$ 6
Medicare B Premium	$1,062	$ 89
Medicare B Deductible	$ 83	$ 7
Medicare B Co-Pay	$ 902	$ 75
Other Miscellaneous	$ 293	$ 24
Dental/Vision/Hearing	$ 388	$ 32
Medicare Supplement (Medigap) F	$2,244	$187
Prescriptions (Medicare Part D)	$1,300	$108
Totals:	$6,631	$551

Every year Fidelity Investments updates and releases results from its annual retiree health care study. The study assumes an average 65-year-old couple, without employer-provided health care, retiring in 2007, with average life expectancy of age 82 for the male and age 85 for the female. As is apparent from the numbers above, the Fidelity Investments study shows that a couple retiring in 2007 would need $215,000 for health care costs during retirement. This figure comprises Medicare Parts B and D premiums, prescription drug out-of-pocket costs, and miscellaneous out-of-pocket costs, including co-payments, co-insurance, and deductibles. There are some gaps in the study that could dramatically change the results. Costs such as nursing homes, long-term care, home health care, dental, health maintenance items, and over-the-counter drugs have not been included. The breakdown according to the Fidelity Study is that 33 percent of this cost will be spent out of pocket on prescription drugs, 35 percent consists of the co-pays, co-insurance, and deductibles, and the remaining 32 percent is used to pay Medicare Part B and D premiums. It also takes into consideration the rapid adjustments of cost due to inflation. Again, remember that these are average costs and could be higher or lower depending on your area costs and choice of plans.

According to the *Journal for Financial Service Professionals,* January 2001, in an article titled "Some Observations About the Senior Citizens' Freedom to Work Act of 2000," 40 percent of the seniors who are now turning 65 will spend a portion of their remaining years in a nursing home. Nursing home costs become an extremely important part of health care costs and must be part of the plan for retirement.

Estimated Long-Term Care Costs	(average national costs)
Home Care Services	$25.32 per hour
Assisted Living Facility	$32,294
Nursing Home Facility	$70,912

As you can see from the chart above, considering long-term care costs or the cost of a long-term care insurance policy is mandatory for planning a comfortable and successful retirement budget.

Insurance Options

This section discusses insurance solutions. The myriad of options available to today's workers ranges from employer-, government-, and union-provided benefits to Medicare, its related supplemental plans, and comprehensive major medical plans purchased by individuals. All of these plans have their positives and negatives, including costs, deductibles, and limitations on benefits and service providers. Health care buyers must determine both which type of plan is right for them and the financial impact on their income in retirement.

Employer-Provided Plans

Employer-provided plans usually have the largest range of plan benefits and plan costs. While some employers pay eligible retirees' health insurance premiums, the costs associated with each plan varies as widely as do the companies that offer the programs. Retirees at some companies may receive comprehensive benefits with no premiums, while others may incur premiums as high as 50 percent of the cost to the employer and benefits may not include any coverage for spouses.

Advantages of retaining plans offered by the employer are that the employee is comfortable with the plan and can continue to see his or her own doctors. Also, the employer usually pays a significant portion of the health plan premiums on behalf of the employee and the premiums are not counted as taxable income to the employee.

Causes for concern include a lack of accountability on the part of employers to maintain current coverage levels and cost sharing, as well as the inability of the employee or retiree to have input into plan changes such as deductibles, provider networks, and plan benefits and costs.

COBRA (Consolidated Omnibus Budget Reconciliation Act)

If an employer does not allow the employee to remain on its plan, the employee may be eligible for COBRA benefits when he or she leaves full-time employment. To offer COBRA benefits, the employer must have employed at least 20 employees. If so, COBRA could be a reasonable option. COBRA gets a bad rap as being too expensive, but the COBRA premium is the actual amount the employer pays for the employee health insurance plan. However, it is true that an employer may surcharge 2 percent for administrative costs; based on a $1,000 premium, this is only $20 per month. COBRA may be an excellent choice, especially for those who have significant illnesses that require ongoing care and those who will become eligible for Medicare within the next 18 months.

For those who have an option of selecting COBRA but are under age 63½, selecting COBRA has its pitfalls. The primary concern is that once COBRA runs out, health care options may be extremely limited and premium costs could be outrageous, especially if health has deteriorated in that time. Those that select COBRA and have major health issues may have to rely on purchasing coverage on a guaranteed issue basis, such as those available through state insurance plans. Other choices include going without insurance or buying a limited expense plan, which may involve taking an excessive amount of risk. Also, it should be noted that many insurance companies do not issue individual plans to applicants over age 63½. The reasons include the costs of issuing a policy and the high risk for the approximately 17 months the individual would be insured.

Individual Health Plans and Major Medical

If a retiree is not eligible for COBRA or employer benefits, he or she has the option to choose an individual health insurance plan, also referred to as major medical insurance. A benefit to a lower cost, high-deductible plan is the ability to couple it with a health savings account (HSA), which allows the participant the opportunity to put away funds for retirement health care needs, pay any present out-of-pocket expenses, and even pay for some long-term care premiums. It also allows the consumer to be the watchdog of his or her own insurance program and provides greater flexibility. The buyer can help control costs by adding or removing features, such as the doctor office co-pay feature, prescription drug card, and higher deductibles. The fewer features added, the lower the premiums will be. For some people, choosing a high-deductible plan makes a lot of sense.

To have an HSA, the insured needs to carry a health insurance plan with a high deductible. On December 8, 2003, President Bush signed a bill into law that allowed for HSAs. The minimum deductible of an HSA-qualified plan is $1,100 for an individual and $2,200 for a family. Out-of-pocket maximum costs, which include deductibles and co-pays, cannot exceed $5,500 for individuals and $11,000 for families in 2007. The deductible, out-of-pocket maximums and HSA contribution limits are inflation adjusted each year. For 2007, the contribution limits are $2,850 for individuals and $5,650 for families, with an option of an additional $800 catch-up contribution for those 55 and older. Legislation passed on December 9, 2006, provided that an individual can participate in an HSA for the maximum contribution even if it is more than the deductible and out-of-pocket limits. While HSAs can be a great insurance planning tool, they are relatively new and greatly underused. The growth and awareness of HSAs is just beginning.

An HSA contribution is tax deductible and allows for tax-free growth of the earnings. The tax-free growth associated with these plans means that money will grow faster, simply due to the fact that the tax is not paid and therefore the entire amount is working for the saver. No taxes are paid on the gain or for qualified distributions. The medical expenses that are paid from the HSA are done so on a tax-free basis and, depending on the consumer's tax bracket and state taxes, could add as much as an additional 40 percent to the purchasing power of the plan.

HSAs have considerable tax advantages. The HSA contribution is considered a tax deduction when it is contributed, regardless of whether the individual itemizes on the federal tax form. This is a huge advantage, since the deduction of medical expenses usually requires that non-self-employed individuals must have exceeded at least 7.5 percent of adjusted gross income (AGI) prior to receiving a deduction. By deducting the money that was put into the HSA and then paying the expense with tax-free dollars, the consumer, in reality, recaptures the capability of having a tax-deductible expense without the hassle. The additional growth in the HSA that may never be taxed is simply an added bonus.

HSAs are flexible. The holder can maintain the HSA if he or she relocates across state lines, has a change in marital status, changes jobs, retires, or changes medical plans. The HSA is independent of the high-deductible plan it supplements, so even if the consumer no longer has a high-deductible plan, he or she may maintain an HSA. The funds can still be used for HSA-qualified medical expenses, but funds cannot be added to the account. However, HSA funds may be transferred from one HSA plan to another. Also, distributions can be made for other dependents even if they are not covered under the high-deductible medical plan. In addition, the insured may be able to transfer moneys from an individual retirement account (IRA) to a qualified HSA. Some restrictions may apply.

An HSA continues after death if a spouse is named as beneficiary of the account and will be treated as though it were the spouse's health savings account. If, however, the account transfers to anyone other than the spouse, the fair market value of the account becomes taxable to the beneficiary.

The HSA allows for coverage not considered under normal health plans. Dental and vision plans usually must be purchased to cover these types of expenses. If desired, distributions from the HSA can be used to pay for this care on a tax-free basis, without itemizing. This capability, depending on the situation, may eliminate the value or need for additional coverage.

One of the biggest, but less advertised, benefits of the HSA is the ability to "take care of business" immediately without waiting for an insurance company. Very few people around have not received a notice of delinquency while waiting for the insurance to take care of a bill. The HSA may reduce or eliminate these problems.

Similar to the HSA is the Archer medical savings account (MSA), which is part of the Medicare Advantage program. The qualifications are very similar to those of the HSA, including a high-deductible plan with no additional insurance, and the policyholder cannot be a dependent on anyone else's tax form. In addition, the MSA holder cannot have another Medicare plan. The restrictions and benefits are the same, as is the portability and capability to pass the moneys on after death.

The primary disadvantage of HSAs is the reluctance of the insured to seek medical care and have expensive tests performed because of the high out-of-pocket expense. Secondarily, moneys removed prior to age 65, if not used for medical purposes, are subject to a 10 percent penalty and the distributed amount is taxed as ordinary income.

When deciding on a major medical plan, buyers will be given the option of choosing an indemnity plan or a managed care plan such as a PPO (preferred provider organization), HMO (health maintenance organization), or POS (point of service) plan, which confine health care to a network of providers. Indemnity plans allow the insured to go the hospital or doctor of choice. The insurance company decides if services received are covered by the policy, or if the charge is reasonable and customary for the procedure performed. There is usually a deductible to be met on an annual basis and then an amount, called co-insurance; where the insured co-pays anywhere from zero percent to 70 percent of the expenses to the out-of-pocket limit. Many plans have zero percent co-insurance options, which may be favorable. Charges above the customary charge are paid by the insured but are not included as part of the deductible or co-pay out-of-pocket limit. Once the out-of-pocket limit is reached, the insurance pays the remaining reasonable and customary charges for the year up to a lifetime maximum. Average lifetime maximums are usually $1 million. With today's skyrocketing health care costs, it is easy to understand how someone could use up the entire maximum on one catastrophic illness. Patients have been known to wipe out most of the limit on their health care with an extended stay in the intensive care unit. Many companies are realizing this issue and increasing the maximum.

A primary difference between indemnity plans and managed care plans is that managed care plans have pre-negotiated fee schedules with a network of providers; indemnity plans do not have a network of providers, and charges are subject to the insurance companies' usual customary and reasonable (UCNR) guidelines. If choice of providers is not an issue, then managed care plans will limit financial surprises and out-of-pocket expenses caused by charges in excess of UCNR guidelines. Due to discounts managed care plans receive from providers, the premiums for managed care plans are usually less expensive.

Financial Tidbit: Consider purchasing an insurance plan with a $2,500 deductible and zero percent co-insurance instead of a typical $500 deductible major medical plan with 20 percent coinsurance to $10,000. The maximum out-of-pocket amounts are the same, yet premium savings from choosing the $2,500 deductible may exceed 25 percent.

Short-Term Major Medical Plans and Limited-Expense Plans

Extreme caution should be exercised when using these types of plans. While many companies refuse to issue these plans to persons 64 and older, there are companies that will. It is common practice for many short-term policies to exclude prescription drugs and pre-existing conditions from coverage. Typically, these policies are issued only for six months and are not renewable. The attraction to short-term policies is simple: They are very affordable, with as much as 50 percent lower premiums than individual or employer-provided insurance plans. Short-term policies also have very few insurance questions, which makes getting approved easier. For those persons within six months of Medicare eligibility, a short-term policy can be a useful and affordable alternative to bridge the gap to Medicare.

Financial Tidbit: Consider purchasing a short-term policy for the six months before enrolling in Medicare. A short-term policy may save you up to 70 percent on your premiums and bridge the gap to Medicare.

Medicare and Medigap

In addition to employer-provided plans and individual plans, government-sponsored plans such as Medicare are an option. Medicare was created in 1965, under President Lyndon Johnson, to address the needs of an elderly population with medical expenses.

Medicare Part A covers in-patient care and is generally paid for through a Medicare tax on payrolls and other government revenues. Medicare Part B covers doctors and most out-patient care. A monthly charge is typically made to Medicare beneficiaries and increases each year based on the inflation index used by Medicare/Centers for Medicare and Medicaid Services (CMS). The premium for Medicare is the same for all beneficiaries with a few exceptions, such as those who may qualify to have some or all of their Medicare Part B premium subsidized due to low-income status and others who may be charged a much higher amount based on above-average incomes.

For those people subject to a surcharge for their Medicare Part B premiums, it is just another cost that must be accounted for. Below is a chart that illustrates the surcharge and those affected,

(See next page)

Chart: Projected Monthly Part B Premium Amounts Based on Income

	Individuals with income of $80,000 or less Married couples with income of $160,000 or less *(25% of program costs)*	Individuals with income between $80,000 - $100,000 Married couples with income between $160,000 - $200,000 *(35% of program costs)*	Individuals with income between $100,000 - $150,000 Married couples with income between $200,000 - $300,000 *(50% of program costs)*	Individuals with income between $150,000 - $200,000 Married couples with income between $300,000 - $400,000 *(65% of program costs)*	Individuals with income above $200,000 Married couples with income above $400,000 *(80% of program costs)*
2007	$98.20	$111.16	$130.61	$150.05	$169.49
2008	$98.20	$124.52	$163.99	$203.47	$242.95
2009	$98.30	$137.62	$196.60	$255.58	$314.56
2010	$102.20	$143.08	$204.40	$265.72	$327.04

Source: NCPSSM calculation based on data from the Annual 2006 Report of the Boards of Trustees of the Federal Hospital Insurance and Federal Supplementary Medical Insurance Trust Funds.

Note: Income thresholds will rise with the consumer price index beginning in 2008.

Enrollment in Medicare Part A usually occurs without any effort from the Medicare beneficiary; however, actual enrollment is necessary for Medicare Part B. The process for enrolling in Medicare may require an appointment at the local social security office three months prior to the Medicare expected effective date. The Medicare effective date is the first day of the month in which the recipient turns 65 years of age. For example, if a birthday were September 15, the Medicare effective date would be September 1. However, an exception to this rule does exist: For those whose birthday is on the first of the month, the Medicare effective date is the first day of the previous month. For example if the birthday were March 1, the Medicare effective date would be February 1 instead of March 1. In addition, there may also be an effective date not related to a birthday in the event the party is receiving Medicare disability benefits. Typically, Medicare Part A and Part B effective dates will be the same, but there are common exceptions. For example, some people may choose to receive their health insurance through their employer plan or their spouse's employer plan and save the money they would pay Medicare for the Part B premium. While there are guidelines and eligibility rules regarding timely enrollment or canceling enrollment in Medicare Part B, this is outside this discussion.

In 2004, because of skyrocketing prices and large gaps in the Medicare system, the Medicare Prescription Drug, Improvements, and Modernization Act (MMA) provided for additional options to supplement Medicare Parts A and B. Medicare+Choice was offered to expand benefits through private health insurance programs like HMOs and PPOs that have made contracts with Medicare. Later, congressional reform changed Medicare+Choice to Medicare Advantage.

Medicare Supplements

Medicare Parts A and B must be in place to qualify for a Medigap policy. Medigap insurance has been under the scrutiny of the federal government more than almost any other type of insurance. These insurance policies are the traditional type of medical insurance. Buyers should always check with their advisors before purchasing a plan. This will ensure that it contains all the elements that are necessary for their situation and that it is approved as a supplement for Medicare.

The cost of Medigap insurance will vary from company to company, even though the benefits may be the same. The premium will also vary based on the age of the applicant. No one can be turned down for the insurance if applied for at age 65, but after that time the window closes, and changing may be difficult if health issues are present. The buyer could be left with a policy that has escalating costs and no other options.

Medicare Part D covers prescription medications and varies in cost depending on which plan is chosen, the prescription drugs to be covered, which insurance company the plan is purchased from, and whether or not the insured receives a low-income subsidy. These plans have a deductible, which is indexed to inflation and may have a co-pay. There is a limit, called a coverage limit, which the plan will pay. Once the coverage limit is reached, the monthly premium must continue to be paid and so must all drug costs until a ceiling is reached. Once the coverage limit is exceeded, catastrophic benefits begin.

Medicare Advantage

Medicare Advantage plans are health plan options approved by Medicare and run by private companies. They are part of the Medicare program and are commonly referred to as "Part C." Medicare pays a set amount for your care every month to these private health plans whether or not you use any services. Payment for covered services is made by the private insurance companies and HMOs that enrolled the member.

The advantage of Medicare Advantage plans is that premiums are low when compared to traditional Medicare supplements and employer-based plans.

The plans, premiums, and benefits are as diverse as the companies that issue them. Unfortunately, CMS has not standardized these plans like Medicare supplements. These plans tend to be confusing and misunderstood, with very little available information. CMS prohibits insurance companies and agents from helping seniors choose among the plans available. Medicare's policies appear to put seniors at a significant disadvantage when trying to find the plan that best suits their needs. Because of the confusion surrounding these plans, it is easy to see why seniors have been skeptical.

Medicare Advantage plans could be the Holy Grail for many people when it comes to finding alternative, effective means of obtaining protection at competitive rates. In most areas, these plans are available with premiums exceeding $100 per month, but in many areas of the country, these plans have $0 monthly premiums. Low-premium plans present good arguments to forgo Medicare supplements and their expensive premiums for what amounts to 20 percent coverage and deductibles being covered in some cases. For those who are competent at mathematics, understand the value of money, and are interested in receiving appropriate value for the many risks they are willing to assume, many Medicare Advantage plans provide compelling opportunities.

Deemed providers are physicians who are aware of the plan you are enrolled in and provide Medicare-approved services. While they do not have to accept you and your plan in the future, they do have to accept your plan's payment if they knew which plan you were enrolled in and still treated you. With deemed providers, the doctors and insurance companies are able to save time and money by not needing to negotiate rate discounts because physicians will use the current Medicare fee schedule.

Keep in mind that just because these plans may have $0 premiums, it does not imply they are free. These plans usually have co-pays and co-insurance provisions that cause the insured to incur some out-of-pocket costs. In some lesser plans, these costs could routinely equal or exceed $5,000 or more a year per person.

There are several different forms of Medicare Advantage plans ranging from PFFSs, PPOs to HMOs, and hybrids thereof, including the newly popular regional PPO plans.

Medicare PFFSs are the least restrictive of the Medicare Advantage plans. Physicians must only agree to accept the terms and conditions of the plan. These plans do not use networks of providers or require referrals.

Medicare PPOs are Medicare Advantage plans with additional restrictions to a network of providers. Benefits, while reduced, are available out of network without a referral, but will result in higher out-of-pocket costs.

Medicare HMOs are Medicare Advantage plans, similar to PPOs, except referrals to specialists are required to receive payment for these services and for care performed out of network. For care received out of network, the insured may have to pay all costs.

Medicare Medical Savings Plans

These plans have not reached widespread acceptance, as many people are hesitant to have a premium and high deductible because other affordable Medicare Advantage options exist.

Medicare medical savings plans do not begin to pay covered costs until you have met the annual deductible.

As with other insurance options, Medicare Part C has both its advantages and disadvantages. Some of the advantages are worldwide coverage for emergencies, low co-pays, and no deductibles, which makes needed medical care affordable. Routine physical exams, vision and hearing benefits, gym memberships, and prescription plans are sometimes included.

Every year during open enrollment periods, you may change your plan from one company to another. Unfortunately, no one is allowed to suggest the best plan for your needs due to CMS guidelines.

Some important disadvantages to keep in mind are restrictions on when you can enroll and change plans, and a lack of quality educational information provided to Medicare beneficiaries from CMS, physicians, insurance companies, and independent insurance agents. Plans can change their benefits each year, which may encourage the insured to change to a different plan, and plans could be canceled, but significant Medicare protections are built in to protect affected Medicare beneficiaries.

There are some people for whom a Medicare Advantage plan would not be a good fit.

Anyone living where most physicians are not willing to accept the plan, and people who suffer from chronic health conditions that require many physician office visits, extension tests, and medical treatments, should consider alternative options.

The problems we are experiencing today are the same types of problems we experienced prior to the standardization of Medicare supplement plans. With a little direction from CMS, standardization of available plans, and marketing guidelines that have the consumer in mind, these plans could become the most prominent senior health plans throughout the country.

Consider the following: Instead of purchasing a Medicare supplement with an average premium of $2,244 per year, consider enrolling in a Medicare Advantage plan with a $2,000 to $3,000 out-of-pocket limit and transferring the much larger risk of long-term care to an insurance company.

For those with the Medicare Advantage policy, a Medigap policy will not pay uncovered bills. The Medicare Advantage program was designed to stand alone. It is necessary to choose Parts A and B Medicare and a supplement, or choose the Medicare Advantage program.

Comparison Tidbit: Before enrolling in a Medicare Advantage plan, have the agent or company walk through sample claims such as cancer and heart by-pass treatments. This will improve your understanding of these plans.

Standalone Specialty Policies

In making plans for health care, it is important not to neglect specialties, including dental, eye refractory, and-long-term care. Several companies offer individual specialty policies that can be integral in a solid health care insurance program.

Dental insurance can be one of the more important, yet most neglected insurances. According to the American Association of Retired Persons (AARP), there is a great deal of evidence that links periodontal disease, which is continuous infection of the gums, to a myriad of serious diseases and medical conditions. Some of the conditions linked are heart disease, diabetes, respiratory problems, and even stroke.

There are still a number of health care costs not covered by any insurance company. Strides have been made to bring well care and preventive care to the public, so some policies may now include benefits for fitness classes and some wellness benefits.

Long-Term Care

There is an additional plan that has, in recent years, changed from a luxury to a vital tool in retirement planning. This type of plan is called long-term care (LTC). One of the main reasons for that change is that care in the final years has altered dramatically. A century ago, the elderly lived in an extended family, with a child, usually a daughter. As the senior aged, the chores lessened and the job of advisor became more the norm. Finally, the child and her family became the caretaker of the parent. Today not only are parents living longer, but miles separate the parents from their children. Women work outside the home, and care taking has become an impossible task.

The reality is that one out of every two people 65 years or older will end up spending some time in a nursing home. Benefits for the nursing home are available through Medicare, but significant limitations and restrictions exist with regard to qualifying for benefits. For instance, for Medicare to authorize payments in a nursing home, you must first be hospitalized three days, require skilled nursing, and have a condition that is expected to improve. The challenge here is that most people in long-term care facilities are not in need of skilled nursing care, but custodial care. The only product that will pay for that type of care is a long-term care policy.

Quality LTC policies usually combine nursing home benefits with home health care benefits, although standalone plans may be available.

Many individuals have not had experience caring for others and are unaware of its destructive impact, both emotionally and financially. Others believe it cannot happen to them.

Another mistake is waiting to purchase LTC until the visible deterioration of aging is seen. Unfortunately, this decision usually leads to permanently putting off covering this exposure once people get older and see how expensive coverage costs become.

A common reason for responsible LTC planning is relieving the undue stress and responsibility that is passed onto family members. A person needing long-term care but who does not reside in a nursing facility most often has to rely on his or her children, spouse, or other family members to provide this care. Often these family members have children of their own, and the struggle to balance the needs of their parents and their children defines the phenomenon referred to as the sandwich generation. Caregivers, in general, suffer a great many stress-related illnesses from trying to wear too many hats at the same time. Social events are balanced between children and care taking, leaving the child to be shortchanged. The caregiver is torn, whether it is between the parent and the child, the parent and the job, or all three: job, parent, and child. The stress related to this can cause premature aging in the caretaker and illness.

The long-term caregiver also has additional out-of-pocket costs. Adjustments to living facilities to make housing handicapped accessible, daytime and replacement caregivers when necessary, and medical equipment for the living area are all expenses that usually are not accounted for when planning for a family member to act as caregiver.

Regardless of whether a family member or a nursing facility is used to provide long-term care, it is important to recognize the accelerating costs of both, and plan accordingly for that cost. In fact, it is important to have an LTC insurance plan in place long before you need it. Once it becomes obvious that the plan is needed, the chances of obtaining any plan are doubtful. The recipients with no insurance will have to pay expenses out of their own pocket. These costs are also growing at an alarming rate, with no end in sight. The cost of nursing facilities has risen year after year. Today, the average cost varies a great deal from city to city, but can be estimated at about $150 to $250 per day.

The best time to purchase LTC insurance, according to study done by Connecticut Partnership for LTC, is prior to the buyer's sixtieth birthday. The study revealed that a 55-year-old that purchased coverage was better off financially than a 75-year-old who waits to buy LTC when both require benefits at age 85.

Many elements go into the pricing of LTC, including features such as home health care, inflation protection, and the elimination period (the length of stay before benefits begin). The biggest cost factor is the age and health of the applicant. Various states offer partnership plans, but a decision must be made whether to get a standard plan or a partnership plan. Partnership plans provide total asset protection in case care is needed longer than the policy pays benefits. While partnership plans are more expensive than traditional plans, they also protect your assets, but not your income. The entire process may sound complicated and confusing, and there is a good reason for that. It is. Understanding the amount necessary, the type of policy, all the intricacies of the policy, the amount of coverage needed, how to pay for the coverage, and when to buy can be made simpler by discussing the issue with a financial advisor or qualified insurance agent.

Financial Tidbit: Consider purchasing an LTC policy with an elimination period of 100 days to coordinate with Medicare and receive a premium discount up to 20 percent.

Additional Expenses

Staying in your own home is an option if you do not require 24-hour medical supervision. This is where home health care comes in, and even though you are living in your own home, the cost can be just as expensive as care received in a nursing home.

Early Planning: Choosing a Plan/Advisor

Now that we have discussed many of the health care options available during retirement, including an examination of LTC, we can walk through the process of choosing a policy along with a financial advisor.

To properly plan for major medical expenses, it is imperative that you understand what costs may be incurred. This means that the individual must take an interest in this subject or put his or her entire financial future in the hands of a trusted advisor.

To make knowledgeable decisions, the retiree must also participate in the process of decision making. An understanding of the products to be purchased, even at minimum levels, is a requisite in the process. The insured must actually read the accompanying brochures, check out the financial ratings of the company, check it out with the states' department of insurance, and work through possible claim situations with the insurance agent. It is important to see the insurance company's list of covered prescription drugs. The time to find out what is covered by an insurance policy is not when the policy is needed, but before it is purchased. A qualified, caring advisor can help you with these tasks and should be able to understand and explain all policy features, limitations, and exclusions. You should feel comfortable with your advisor of choice.

Friends and family members are among the best resources to locate an insurance agent; a trusted financial advisor, especially one who has had claims and service experience with the recommended agent, is another good referral source. Prior to retiring, you should interview agents who specialize in health care with an emphasis in Medicare coverage. The ideal agent will have access to all of the Medicare products, including Medicare supplements, Medicare Advantage, HMOs, PPOs, FSSPs, Medicare prescription plans, LTC, and other senior health plans. This is not the time to hire an agent with little knowledge or limited access to the senior health insurance marketplace. Good service makes absolutely all the difference when it comes to the complexity of products, services, and claim issues arising from Medicare insurance plans, so avoiding poor service should be one of the measures in choosing a representative.

Retirement is not the time to go directly to a company for insurance needs. You need to consult a trusted advisor. When purchasing through the mail, over the phone, or via the Internet, remember that confidential information is being transferred through less than secure means. Great caution should be taken to avoid a stolen identity.

When dealing with an insurance professional, especially an independent agent, many companies and products and services are available. These agents can shop and compare to meet the customer's needs. The retirement years are not the time to become a self-taught do-it-yourselfer. Medicare has never been as complex as it is today and changes occur every year, sometimes several times during the year. Professional agents who specialize in the Medicare area are a good resource. Using them should help you reap Medicare rewards.

Once a consultant is chosen, it is time to begin planning. Financial planning for health care in retirement should not begin at retirement, but much earlier. When establishing a savings plan, it should also be anticipated how and when future medical expenses and premiums are more likely to occur and what income and assets will be used to meet those expenses. The sooner you start, the easier it is to achieve success. A good financial plan for expenses in the retirement years is essential. Retirement money is easier to accumulate when savings begin at an early age.

A Process for Shopping for Individual Health Insurance Plans

While these guidelines apply to the process of finding a qualified advisor, they also apply to do-it-yourselfers.

Shopping should begin by checking with the department of insurance for the state in which the health care buyer lives and inquiring about which insurance company's plans are sold most often in the appropriate area. Sometimes bigger is better, especially when it comes to health insurance. However, it is important to check company ratings. A company that is highly rated with the major rating agencies, including AM Best, Standard & Poor's, and Moody's, tends to be stronger and will be able to meet demands for claim payments. While lower rated companies may have lower premiums and attractive benefits, their lower financial rating is a warning sign that they may not be able to meet their financial obligations now or in the future. It may not be worth the headaches of slow claims, poor service, or radical premium adjustments to get a little lower premium for a short period of time. HMOs may not be rated; this is not a common occurrence. This does not mean they are financially unstable, but a little different form of insurance. It is a much riskier proposition to choose low-rated or unrated companies selling traditional health insurance than highly rated companies that have a history, and probably a future, of strength and rapid claim payment. The more uncertainty that is removed, the more accurate results should be.

A Health Care Planning Checklist:

How should you go about making certain you have the right health care solution? You must consider all of the options and obtain as much information as possible to make an informed decision.

1. Understand fully your current situation, including costs, providers, and spousal coverage.

2. Analyze all of your options, including employer plans, individual plans, COBRA, and Medicare.

3. Implement your plan.

4. Monitor your health care program for changes and improvements.

Review/Conclusion

In this chapter we have provided an explanation of the costs of health care in retirement, some options for funding these expenses, and a few questions to ask a financial advisor to help make the decision on an insurance policy an educated one. However, these are just guidelines, and it is still important to employ the services of a qualified financial advisor.

Proper health care planning may be more important to a person's future financial well-being than the choice between a traditional or Roth IRA. The decision is far more important than whether an international load fund or a no-load index fund is purchased. It is definitely much more important than A-shares, B-shares, or a fee-based account, and yet it seems people spend more energy debating those issues. Health care decisions could be the most important decisions a retiree makes... they never should be taken lightly.

Words for the Wise

1. Individual health policies should be applied for at least 45 to 60 days prior to the date you want coverage to begin. This will allow time to make sure that ID cards arrive prior to the coverage effective date. It will also allow some time to find alternative coverage if not approved by the first company of choice.

2. It is important to make certain that you understand the policy that is purchased and its limitations.

3. The purchaser should beware of limited expense plans, typically offered through an association, many of which are sold as comprehensive major medical plans. Frequently, these types of plans pay a small percentage of the actual costs incurred. Frequently, they are referred to as feel-good plans, because the clients feel good knowing they have some insurance. In actuality they may end up broke once they get ill. The same feeling could have been gained without one cent paid out in premiums. While it may be a different level of broke, not having money still means the same thing in the end. No matter what level, broke is broke.

Chapter 13

Business Succession Planning

Contributing Author Thomas C. Schmidt, Sr.

Business Succession Planning

L et your mind wander back in time to when you first started your business, perhaps even further, to when your business was just a dream or a sketch on a napkin. Think about all the time that has passed since then. So much of you and perhaps your family has been poured into that dream. Now the business you dreamed of may very well be one of your largest assets.

The business you built has become one of your major assets and most likely your major source of income, so what do you do now? You are not ready to retire, yet you realize that you will not be working forever. It is time to think about how you will protect the wealth that you have built and keep it going when you leave. If it is a family business, you must concern yourself with both family and business. Even if it is not a family business, there are clients and employees you probably want to protect through continuation of the business.

Let us shift gears just a bit now. Instead of owning the business, assume that you have been with the company so long that you cannot imagine yourself anywhere else. The owner will someday retire to pursue other interests. Where does that leave you? Would you rather have a secure future, comfortable that the business will still be around to provide for you, or would you rather roll with the punches and see what happens?

You might prefer to become part of a plan that will allow you to take over the business and buy it from the owner.

Whether you are the owner looking for the right way to protect what you have built and have it provide for you and your family or you are the key employee who wants to see the business continue to provide for your income and retirement building, the best alternative seems to be a well-designed business succession plan.

A well-designed business succession plan is the proactive response to your desire for leaving your business legacy.

What Is Business Succession Planning?

Business succession planning is the process that one goes through to ensure the orderly and efficient transition of a business. At the time of your death or retirement, your business will go through a transition; however, if it is an unplanned transition it may not result in the business legacy that you care to leave behind.

Business succession planning generally involves two major areas, both of which are crucial to the success of the transition and the future success of the business: (1) the transfer of the management and operations of the business and (2) the financial aspects of the transfer. It is only logical that the first item be addressed first since that person or persons will be party to the financial aspects of the transfer.

The transfer of the operations and management of the business requires that the business owner identify who the successors will be. Whether the business is a family business or not, the successor or successors may not be readily obvious to the owner. This becomes even more important when you consider that short of an all-cash sale, the execution of the succession plan is the mechanism by which the owner will extract the value from the business. To understand how sticky these situations can be, consider some of the following scenarios:

- Father owns the business and two sons work in the business. Father also has a daughter who does not work in the business. Both sons wish to remain in the business. The daughter has no interest in being involved in the business. Now imagine that the daughter would like to receive her eventual value of the business in cash.

- Father owns and son works in the business. Another son owns a competing company. Brothers do not get along particularly well and no one can imagine them working together.

- Owner has three children, none of whom work in the business; nor are they interested in getting involved in the business. Owner has a long-time trusted employee he would like to take over the business. The employee is a good businessman, although he does not have the cash to purchase the business.

- Husband and wife own the business together and each has children from previous marriages involved in the business. The wife also has a child from a previous marriage that is not involved in the business. Both the husband and wife would like the business to stay in the family and will have to decide who will run the business after the transfer. This might be further complicated if the children involved in the business have similar and not complementary skills.

These are just a few examples of the many situations and issues that you may face when planning the transition of management responsibilities of a business. Consider the reality of your own situation and the various issues that you may have to face. Underlying that are the many issues related to structuring a deal that meets the owner's expectations in an orderly and efficient manner. These situations can be further complicated when other people are added to the equation, when individual personalities and agendas are included or the owner thinks that he or she will live forever. The list of possible issues to consider is almost endless. The good news is that with a sound planning process, none of these situations should be insurmountable. With proper advance planning and competent advice, nearly all conceivable issues can be handled in a manner that will allow for the achievement of the ultimate goal, an orderly and efficient business transfer.

The second part of the succession planning involves the financial aspects of the transfer, which are equally important to the process and can often seem much more complicated. Depending on the issues involved, this part can in fact be more complicated. Again, with advance planning, the issues can be addressed so that the goals of the business owner are met.

For the succession plan to work for both the business owner and the successor, a deal must be structured that not only creates the most value for the owner but also allows the successor to continue to operate the business at a profit. This requires consideration of many different areas, including the tax ramifications to the buyer and seller, the cash needs of the seller, and the cash resources of the buyer. It also requires carefully constructed documentation to ensure that all parties are protected. As stated earlier, business succession planning is a process, and a process involves many moving parts and steps to be completed. Therefore, it is wise to have already assembled a group of advisors to ensure a greater chance of success in the execution of the plan. If you have not assembled such a group, consider doing so.

The team concept is evident in all areas of our society and is accepted as a logical means of harnessing skills across multiple disciplines to achieve a common purpose, much the same as an NFL owner needs to have many positions filled to produce a winning team. The investment in assembling the team is required to gain the spoils of success. Suppose you are the owner of the NFL team and your goal is to win the Super Bowl. You hire the brightest football mind to coach the team. How far can he go on his own? If he adds a quarterback, perhaps the best in the league, how far can they go together? It will take a full complement of players to create the success you deserve. Some players on your team might include:

- Financial advisor/consultant
- Certified public accountant
- Attorney (business, tax and estate)
- Investment banker/business broker
- Facilitator/business consultant

Any of these team members could perform more than one function in the process; it is only important to ensure that all expertise you need is adequately covered with competent advisors.

Now is the time to get started for many reasons. Principal among them is that you do not want the business to be transferred on less than your terms. You provided the blood, sweat, and tears to build the business, and you should have your objectives met in the transfer of the business. Not to mention, a business sold under distress conditions usually sells for a distress price. Succession planning is a process that should be expected to take some time to design and implement. An additional time factor that will generally come out of this process is a period during which the successor can be groomed for the important role that will keep your business going and provide you with the financial benefit for which you worked.

It is hard to determine the amount of time you will need for your particular business situation, but you can almost be assured that your process will take more time than you currently think it will.

There is another reason to think about this now, even though you might be young, healthy, and not close to considering retirement. Death or retirement may not create the only times that a business will be passed on to a successor. The possibility of a disability without death is a real threat, and if succession planning is ignored or the plan only makes allowances for death or retirement of the owner, an unintended disaster could be created. The need for continuing income without a plan to protect it might end with the loss of the business without sufficient reward. This could have a devastating effect on your life, your lifestyle, and your family. Whether the event that triggers the transfer is retirement, death, or disability, the advisable way for the transfer to take place is according to your plan.

There is always an alternative plan to taking the time, expense, and perhaps a bit of pain to do it now on your terms. That plan is one that will be implemented by the state, the judge, or your executor. That is certainly not the one that you and your family deserve or the one that you want to leave.

The Structure of the Deal
Now that the need for succession planning is evident and you have started the process, the time will come to consider the options for structuring the deal. The many issues that need to be considered when constructing the deal should be revealed as a result of discussions and meetings with your team.

Some of the issues to be discussed and considered in the deal are listed below, but not in any particular order:

Price. In a pure sale to an outsider, the issue of price is a bit easier. It will be predicated on some form of market value and will be driven by the desire to get as much for the business as you can.

In a transaction where you are planning the succession of your business to either insiders or family members, the overriding drivers are generally different. In these instances, the deal is generally structured within the confines of the cash flow of the business.

Tax Considerations. There are many tax considerations in structuring the deal that affect both the buyer and the seller.
To the buyer, there are tax issues that have to do with the allocation of the purchase price. Purchase price can be allocated to hard assets being acquired, services to be performed, or certain intangibles such as goodwill, patents, and other intellectual property. Within the range of reasonableness, there are many different categories and methods by which the purchase price can be allocated. Often, the benefit of a particular allocation can be a detriment to the other party. The goal is to find an allocation that as efficiently as possible meets the goal of successfully planning the transfer of the business. Expect that most items need give and take at some level to arrive at a mutually acceptable solution. The discussion above relates to a purchase of assets of the business. If the transaction is a stock purchase, there are additional tax considerations to both the buyer and the seller.

The seller will have tax considerations to deal with from both the income tax area and the estate tax area. The income tax situation of the seller will also be affected differently in a stock sale vs. an asset sale. In an asset sale, much of the seller's tax issues will also revolve around the purchase price allocation. With regard to estate taxes, the business succession planning is really inseparable from the owner's estate plan. Another significant reason for going through the process sooner rather than later is to provide sufficient time to structure the transfer and implement the plan as needed to efficiently manage the owner's estate taxes. There are many techniques to assist in managing the estate taxes of the owner that can be used in conjunction with structuring the deal. The estate tax and the related gift tax cover items (e.g., cash, property, business interests, retirement funds) that are passed along during one's lifetime, as well as at death. As part of business succession planning and estate planning, be sure to get advice on techniques that can be used even though the techniques may be outside the scope of the business transfer. If the business owner is married, be sure to plan for both spouses, as the estate tax is individual since each person has an estate. The income tax issues and the estate tax issues need to be balanced so that an overall tax minimization plan can be designed that still allows for a win-win deal.

Even though the estate tax goes away in 2010, plenty of planning is still necessary. If you die in 2010 and avoid estate taxes altogether, income tax issues will be created on the inherited assets. Finally, the absence of the estate tax, according to current legislation, is only a one-year event, as the estate tax will return in 2011 in a much more burdensome manner than it leaves us in 2010

These discussions are not specifically directed to the family business vs. the non-family business. Keep in mind, however, that succession planning for a family business may involve many people and personalities. This is yet another reason to address it early so that whatever the owner decides to implement as the succession and estate plan can be absorbed by all those involved. In both succession planning and estate planning, both mortality and change need to be discussed. These topics, mortality and change, usually generate feelings that require psychological adjustment and time for acceptance.

For our purposes here, let us assume that the succession planning is ultimately a transfer to family, employee, or other handpicked successor. In making this assumption, we will ignore issues and ramifications of a traditional sale of a business, which involve higher market valuation expectations. If the exit strategy is the sale of the business to an unrelated, open market buyer, other planning considerations specific to that type of transfer should be addressed. Again, this should also be done with the proper team, as there are tax, estate, and retirement issues to consider. Since this succession planning is more of a preferential transfer, consideration must be given to both the seller's needs and the ability of the business to pay the price and remain in business. Regardless of how the deal is structured, the business itself will likely be the major source of repayment.

The options available to transfer the business are many and each has its own issues related to taxes, overall cost, and risk to the parties involved.

Some methods to consider are described in the following paragraphs, although not in the detail that you would need to fully consider and choose the best option. These methods, although not totally exhaustive, provide highlights and ideas that you may discuss more fully with the appropriate advisors.

Transfer by Sale of Stock

The successor purchases the stock from the owner. This would be done with resources of the buyer or with financing secured by the buyer. The downside to the buyer if financing is used is that there is no tax benefit to the buyer on the repayment, which effectively increases the overall cost of the purchase.

Transfer by Gift of Stock

Outright gift of the stock to the successor could have estate/gift tax implications. Currently, a donor may make a tax-free gift to an individual of $12,000 per year, or $24,000 per year if spousal gift splitting is available. If the value of the stock is too great, it could take too long to transfer the business, assuming only the annual exclusion amount is used.

To exceed that amount in any year is possible, although it could have serious estate tax implications and also create other estate planning hurdles. There are also tax issues relative to the buyer in such a situation. Consult your tax advisor before proceeding with this method.

Use of Stock and/or Cash as Compensation

Instead of gifting, the owner could use stock and/or cash as additional compensation to the successor if the business has sufficient cash to support it. This will provide the successor with ownership interest or additional cash with which to purchase the business at the designated time. However, this additional compensation, whether stock or cash, is fully taxable to the employee (successor) in the year it is received. If it were stock alone, it could cause a cash burden on the employee for the additional taxes. This additional compensation may or may not be tax deductible to the employer (business owner).

Stock Options or Restricted Stock

Stock options or restricted shares of stock can be issued and used to transfer minority ownership to the successor. Each of these options has tax considerations that need to be addressed. Also, separate rules that apply to options and restricted shares need to be considered as well. Potential tax burdens are associated with these methods, which might increase the overall cost of the purchase.

Buy-Sell and Cross-Purchase Agreements

Using one of these methods would necessitate the transfer of a minority interest, by some method, to the successor. The agreement would then allow the successor to acquire the remainder interest from the owner at some future date, usually at the death of the owner. This would allow the continuation of the business after the owner's death, provide the financial resources to the estate and heirs of the owner, and almost ensure that there would be no interference from the estate or heirs of the owner. This is usually funded by an insurance policy on the life of the owner, paid for by either the business or the successor depending on the design. This allows some tax advantages to the successor at the time of death. Whether it is a buy-sell or a cross-purchase depends on the number of business owners and the number of successors.

Transfer by Will or by Trust
If done by will, the business would transfer to the successor through probate at the death of the owner according to the terms of the will. This can be risky. For example, the transfer could be worked out and agreed to by both parties and then later changed by the owner without any knowledge of or recourse to the successor. Being named in the will gives no rights to the successor during the lifetime of the owner. Another risk to the successor is that just receiving the business through the will makes a potential challenge by some other party (heir) a messy and expensive proposition. Many considerations should be discussed and examined before this option is chosen. The owner could set up a living trust and then transfer the business into the trust, with the successor as the beneficiary of the trust. The living trust is more efficient for the continuation of the business at the death of the owner. It does warrant mentioning that the owner can change the trust just as the will can be changed. The trust does not become irrevocable until the death of the owner.

Stock Redemption
This method can combine portions of various other methods to achieve a workable alternative. The first step here is for the successor to acquire a minority interest by some means. This could be done by a gifting arrangement or the successor could acquire the interest for cash if that is an option. If the successor acquires the interest with cash, a discounted price

could be justified since a minority interest value is generally discounted due to the minority owner's inability to exert enough influence to control the business in any way. That represents the "disadvantage" to the owning minority interest holder that justifies a lower valuation. Then, the owner completes a total redemption of his shares in the business. This is a redemption of shares back to the company and can be handled with cash if sufficient cash is in the business to do so. This would allow the owner to completely cash out of the business, and that would conclude the financial ties between the owner and the successor. This transaction, the redemption, is a taxable event to the business owner. If all the cash is not available in the business or the owner wishes to manage the tax burden, the redemption by the owner could be structured as an installment sale.

Installment Sale

There are various ways to twist and combine the installment sale process to achieve your stated goals. The straightforward installment sale is to simply transfer the ownership in the stock or assets for some cash and a promise to pay the remainder. In the case of the sale of either stock or assets, a taxable event to the seller has occurred. The gain will be recognized over the term of the repayment, spreading the tax over that time as well. There are tax issues related to both current income and estate taxes that should be considered when evaluating this option. The owner has some flexibility in the interest rate charged provided a minimum rate, as prescribed by the Internal Revenue Service (IRS), is charged. The flexibility in this rate is useful when attempting to manage the repayments within the cash flow constraints of the business. There are also potential tax implications to the buyer that should be addressed in the analysis. If this is a family business, care should be given in using this method. There should be a longer range view in this case, as special rules apply to installment sales between related parties.

Self-Canceling Installment Note

This is a twist on an installment note that allows it to act in a manner similar to a private annuity. These are useful instruments, although they have been scrutinized by the IRS in recent years. Because of this, it is important that a self-canceling installment note be designed properly with sufficient documentation to support the proper use of this method. The benefit of this to the buyer is that if the seller dies before the full payment is made, the outstanding balance owed by the buyer is canceled. To the seller, the outstanding balance of the loan is not included in the gross estate. Although the balance is not included in the owner's estate, the untaxed capital gain is generally taxed as income to the owner's estate at the time of the owner's death. To avoid issues with the note, there needs to be some premium (price or interest) attached to the cancellation feature and the length of the note (term) cannot exceed the life expectancy of the note holder.

Transfer by Installment Loan to a Defective Grantor Trust

This method uses both the trust feature and an installment sale to transfer the interest. As a trust transfer, the grantor names the beneficiary of the trust and the grantor generally remains the trustee. The stock of the business is sold to the trust on an installment basis with an interest rate charged that usually matches the IRS guidelines. Because the trust should not just include the stock of the business, it is advisable to fund the trust with other assets, generally cash, so that the interest can be paid back independent of the success of the business. Because the trust is irrevocable, the value of the trust is not included in the owner's estate. The trust should be made defective for income tax purposes and not for estate and gift tax purposes. Because of this, the trust itself is not taxable for income tax purposes as the income of the trust is taxed to the grantor. The rules regarding this method require that it be properly drafted and adequately funded for it to be a bona fide transaction. When using a transaction method such as this, you will truly come to know and appreciate the value of the team process.

Other options not discussed here may be worthy of discussion with your team to determine if one may be a viable method for your transaction, including:

- Employee stock ownership plan
- Stock recapitalization plan
- Stock split-up
- Private annuity
- Family limited partnership
- Leveraged buyout/outside financing

In the case of the family business, other potential issues may need to be addressed, such as in-laws, divorces, and other family matters. Some of these issues need to be handled as honestly as possible to avoid conflict during this process. The matter of passing on the business could also be used by the owner/parents to try to influence behavior. While they may find that they cannot create a certain behavior in the manner that they wish, they are the owners of the business and they get to decide how the business will be left. This is not much different than using the estate planning process to attempt to elicit certain behavior. In either case, the effort might come with consequences. This could also be the case in a non-family environment, although the lack of emotional entanglement and familial attachment may allow the non-family person to take an altogether different position.

Because of issues such as these and a need for this process to be open and honest, you can follow certain procedures that can be made part of the process. This will create a very personal walk through the past for some people, and almost assuredly people have their own thoughts about the outcome and how it should be achieved. This could be coupled with the fact that the owner has been "The Man" for so long that out of respect or fear no one wants to lay their cards on the table without knowing what everyone has. This leads to a methodology that requires a commitment on the part of the owner as well as all the other parties involved. This is when an outside advisor can provide objectivity, reason, and order to working through the process. This advisor or consultant will set the outline of this discovery phase with the owner or owners as well as identify the persons who will be involved (e.g., spouse, children, in-laws, trusted employees). An individual interview will be conducted with each of the participants during which they will be informed of the process that the owner will be going through as well as this part of the process that they are being included in. They will be allowed to air all of their views on what should happen and how. This would include what they identify as potential pitfalls and hidden opportunities as well as their uninhibited view of the process. It is important that they have the freedom to speak their mind without fear of reprisal. This is information gathering and not a spy mission for the owner. After all of this phase is completed, the next phase will entail all the individuals getting together at the same time for roughly the same discussion. This is best done off site and in a neutral location, such as a hotel, a corporate retreat center, or a similar place where everyone feels at ease to continue the discussions that began in private. The advisor is the moderator and facilitator for the event, which should create a more comfortable setting than if the boss moderated. The goal of the entire process is to come out the other end with a still-viable business that will continue to the benefit of all those involved. To achieve that, the open and honest discussion required is easier to accomplish with an outsider facilitating. Ground rules will be in place to protect the individuals as well as keep the discussions focused on the task. These discussions may have the propensity to break down into gripes and complaints that participants have harbored and, to the extent that they are not on task, participants should not be allowed to simply gripe or complain. If, however, the gripes or complaints indicate the need to address specific issues, it would be wise to work through those issues in the proper setting. At the end of these discussions, the information gathered can be logically assembled and presented to the owner so that the owner has valuable information with which to discuss how to proceed with the business succession planning. What might come from this is better insight by the owner into people and roles they can play that perhaps were not clear before. It should also produce ideas and thoughts regarding the business itself that can be used to make the business stronger regardless of the succession planning process. To that end, any new ideas or suggestions that will strengthen or grow the business might very well be additional protection for the owner, since the continuation and growth of the business is most likely the way that the owner will receive the value from the business.

As you can see, there are many variables and many options for structuring a transfer to achieve an orderly and efficient transition. Accomplishing this requires the combined skills of a team that covers all the necessary disciplines. This is a critical item as there are some very technical legal and tax issues to be handled, and it is always wise to seek the counsel of outside advisors in these circumstances. Many issues must be considered, including the source of funding, numerous tax matters, personalities, and, ultimately, the wants and needs of the seller and the buyer. As mentioned above, some methods are combinations of alternatives and additional methods can be combined to achieve the real and ultimate objective, an orderly and efficient transfer of the business.

Chapter 14

The Seven Habits of Highly Successful Seniors

Contributing Author Charles J. Barley

Back to School Is Scary and Intimidating for Adults

Ask teachers and they will tell you how much they learn from their students. We have often heard that the best way to learn something is to try to teach it yourself. There are some students who don't care how much you know until they know how much you care. We also learn that teaching adults who may not have been in a classroom for more than 30 years can be difficult. It may be hard for them to communicate in a classroom full of strangers. There is a big intimidation factor when you have to register; you receive a thick book, and you are sitting in classroom chairs next to other adult students. So, our team tries to lighten up the room with a few stories about previous students and some of the funny, emotional, or "wow" experiences they had. We also offer rewards for questions or answers. We stimulate the discussion with an assortment of mini-chocolate bars. If they participate, they get an opportunity to select a reward from the jar. This system really helps to bring them out of their shell and get them more comfortable with the surroundings. We have a lot of fun with this idea. You can't believe how excited our choc-a-holics get over this little jar of rewards.

Do you remember the stock market "crash" on Monday, October 19, 1987? The Dow Jones Industrial Average plummeted by 508 points in one day[1]. That's 22 percent in a single day. It was a day of mass confusion. The financial professionals of the time were shocked. Investors were scared to death. Our phone lines were burning up with calls from clients who seemed to be panic stricken. It was very frightening. It reminded me of Scarlet O'Hara in the movie *Gone with the Wind*. As she stood in the ashes of her burned-down house, Tara, she gritted her teeth, sifted the ashes through her hands, and said "I will rebuild and NEVER be poor again." In the depths of her despair, commitment was born; the commitment to rebuild and never look back.

With the 1987 crash and seeing the panic and fear in clients' eyes, our commitment was reborn. We wanted to educate our clients. We decided that an educated client was a better prepared client. Educated clients could better handle market fluctuation, so we began CPI Seminars. We taught in classrooms, churches, colleges, and community centers. We provided educational information about the stock market and helped our clients get a grip on what risks they could expect if they started to invest in equities. We believe that "when you know, you fear no situation!" Not knowing and not understanding the historical cycles of the market can be very scary!

The Dirty Four-Letter Words

Our classes were structured. We provided a 150-page, well-illustrated workbook, and both spouses of married couples were invited. They paid a fee of $39. We talked about planning and discussed taxes, interest rates, and different products like stocks, bonds, and mutual funds. The questions on the minds of our students were, "How much did it earn?" and "How much did it gain?" It was very interesting how many of our students wanted to discuss the rewards. We, however, had to bring them back to earth and discuss the dirty four-letter words: risk, loss, fear, and pain. You could see the smiles disappear from their faces as we brought up the stock market crash of 1987 and tried to relay the fear and pain we saw in our clients' eyes that week.

On the last night of our class, we would ask our students to complete a survey. This form included questions like:

1) What are your financial priorities, both short term (3-5 years) and long term (10-15 years)?

2) Where do you see yourself financially in five years?

3) What do you reasonably expect your investments to earn annually?

From this survey and after reviewing hundreds of client priorities over the years, we were able to identify the "Seven Habits of Highly Successful Seniors," and that is the subject of this chapter.

The Seven Habits of Highly Successful Seniors is a pattern or a process that the successful individuals or couples in our classrooms would follow. They developed habits over the years that they applied to their own financial structure to become financially successful. If you look around your neighborhood, you can spot them. These are your neighbors whose yards and homes are always well maintained. Their lawns are cut regularly, shrubs trimmed, homes painted. They are truly a homeowner with pride in ownership. You will spot these highly successful seniors in your communities and churches. They are always well dressed, fit and trim, and have a smile on their faces. They stand out in a crowd. You can see that they have a goal, and they are pursuing their dreams. They look confident, have a great attitude, and walk 25 percent faster with their shoulders back because they know exactly where they are going.

As a teacher, it is very difficult to stand in the front of a classroom full of adults and try to guess who the millionaires are, but when they have completed their surveys and answered all the questions, it was very easy to spot the successful seniors, and that brings us to habit Number One.

Habit One:
Develop Financial Goals and Objectives

If you have never done this before, you might find it difficult at first. It may take you some time. You may need some help and guidance to get started. You may need some examples because you never thought of doing this before. This, however, is the first and most important link in the chain of becoming financially successful. You must have a plan, a blueprint to work with. Can you imagine:

- A contractor trying to build a house without a blueprint?

- A general going into battle without a battle plan?

- A start-up business without a business plan?

If you don't have a goal post or a goal line, how will you know if you've scored? If you can't keep score, how will you know if you are winning?

As we start the financial planning process, there are three simple questions you must answer. You must ask yourself:

1) What do I want?

2) When do I want it?

3) What do I have to put toward it?

What Do You Want?

Often, a couple has never communicated with each other on their dreams or financial goals and objectives. When planning for retirement, I have discovered that when I ask the questions in our initial interview, they are hearing and addressing the issue for the first time. They haven't made any plans. They haven't even discussed it with each other. They don't know what they want. They seem to be content drifting along like a ship without a rudder...being tossed back and forth by life, just waiting to get to age 65 and then retire to pasture. These individuals are not in charge. They are not in control of their destiny, and they are being controlled rather than taking control. They are living in the past as our parents did when the man of the house would work the same job to age 65. He would retire and receive social security and a small pension and would never consider working again. They put their affairs in order and expected to die within five years. It's not that way anymore! We are a different society now. We are highly mobile. We are not locked into a pension plan as our parents experienced. We have 401(k)s that are profitable, we have individual retirement accounts to supplement our own retirement. We are taking control, and we are not depending on the federal government to provide for us through Welfare or Medicaid programs. We live in better times, where medical advances have increased our life expectancy. The fastest growing part of our society is the 85 and older group[2]. In most communities today, you will find individuals in their late 90s and some over 100.

The 1950 census confirmed that there were only about 4,000 people in the United States who were 100 years old or older. Today, 57 years later, there are more than 55,000 individuals in the United States 100 years old or older. In fact, the United States has more centenarians than any country in the world. Japan is second, with only 25,000 centenarians. By

2050, it is estimated that the United States alone could have as many as one million centenarians[2].

So what's the point? The point is that we are living longer, and we will need to have our money work harder to assure ourselves that we will not run out of money before we run out of life. That requires planning!

Brain Buster

A Brain Buster is a question that we ask our students after we blow a whistle to be sure they are paying attention. If they get the right answer, they get a special reward like a gift certificate to a restaurant or book store. We ask questions such as:

What are the three most important consuming worries of our seniors today?

1) Running out of money

2) ...

3) Good health

This is a good question. The students seem to get one and three but have trouble with number two, which is loss of independence[3]. If I have to tell them the answer, the prize carries over to the next Brain Buster.

With the possibility looming large that we could become centenarians, we must get serious and develop a financial plan with goals that allow our assets to grow and keep pace with or exceed the cost of inflation and taxes to provide for ourselves as we grow older. We cannot depend on our government to take care of us. It shouldn't have that responsibility. Sure, if you have worked for more than 40 years, contributed to social security, and paid your taxes, you may feel that you are entitled to lifetime benefits. Well, with the exception of social security, that is not so. Our tax dollars pave roads, pay the military, and provide health care for the helpless, aged, blind, and disabled.

Oh sure, it is never enough and our government does a lousy job administering our tax dollars, but it is what it is. Let this be your motivation to become financially self-sufficient when you are ready to retire. It's time for you to fish or cut bait. You will be faced with two very important decisions:

1) Am I *financially* prepared?

2) Am I *physiologically* prepared?

Each of these life-changing events is discussed separately. If you decide you want to retire but don't know if you can afford it, a good financial planning process that can help is comparing a "before retirement budget" and an "after retirement budget." This should produce the specific information you need to help you make your decision. By far, the financial preparedness is much easier to determine and is more cut and dried than getting physiologically prepared. That is another story.

Individuals have been programmed to work. When you take away their work, it creates a large vacuum in their lives and perhaps a feeling of uselessness. If these feelings aren't discussed and considered before retirement, it could be emotionally devastating. If you don't plan properly and do not have something to look forward to, retirement may mean "getting ready to die." On the other hand, we at Capital Planning Institute have helped clients retire properly. Some wonder how they ever had time to work. Their life is exciting. They are busy. They are volunteering for work in their community and/or church. They are teaching, changing careers, or starting a new business. It's beautiful to see how happy they are with their new-found freedom. These people are truly "getting ready to live" and move up to the next level of their life. They are the people who have the right frame of mind to get the most out of their lives and may be good candidates to live to become centenarians. The first habit, developing financial goals and objectives, can put you on the right track, help you retire successfully, and make the next chapter of your life very exciting.

Habit Two:
Establish a Time Horizon

Remember, you must answer three important questions:

- What do I want?

- When do I want it?

- What do I have to put toward it?

This paragraph deals with the second question, When do you want it? Your time horizon is a very important guideline for financial planners. They must know your deadline. When do you want to retire? Are you in the *red zone?* The *red zone* is five years before you retire or five years after you retire. How far are you looking into the future? Are you planning for the short term (3-5 years) or long term (10-15 years)? With this information in hand, your financial planner can make recommendations to fit your time horizon. If your time horizon is the rest of your life, as it should be, your financial planner will be able to help you select investments that may perform the best within your risk tolerance level.

When you are determining your time horizon, you also have several timetables to consider. The first is social security. When will you start your social security payments? Will it be early at age 62 or at your full retirement age? If you chose early retirement, you can start your social security income stream as soon as you are age 62. However, to receive your full benefit, you may have to wait until you are age 67. There is a graded scale that goes back to age 65 depending on the year you were born. Individuals born between 1943 and 1954 will have to wait until they reach age 66 before they can receive their full benefit. Whether or not you take an early social security payment may depend on your employment situation. If you plan to work another few years, you are probably better off waiting until you are age 65 when you can avoid loosing any of your social security benefit because of your earned income.

Another timetable to be aware of is the required minimum distribution (RMD) from your individual retirement account (IRA). If you have a traditional IRA, you must start taking distributions when you reach age 70½. Your financial plan should include both your social security timetable and planning for your required minimum distribution.

So, if you can answer this question, your plan will be on track and ready to execute as you anticipate.

When are you planning to start using your assets? How much time do you have to help your portfolio grow to the point where you will have enough capital to provide the income that you want over the balance of your lifetime? We typically plan to age 95. With life expectancies increasing, we don't want you to worry about running out of income. If we overestimate, you won't be upset, but if we underestimate and you run out of money, shame on us! That's why a good financial plan will include your time horizon. We need to know what you want in the short term (3-5 years) and long term (10-15 years). Perhaps this is something that you haven't given much thought too. If that's the case, your financial planner must bring you to a decision or make assumptions that are acceptable and reasonable.

What do you have to put toward it? Taking an inventory of your assets when you begin to prepare a financial plan is very important. We spend a substantial amount of time during our initial interview to get facts up front. When we list your assets, we need to know who owns what. If it is joint ownership, what percentages does each owner own? Are the assets liquid? If more than one property is involved, will any of these properties have to be liquidated at retirement or death? What will the total liquid assets be at retirement and what income will they provide? Is there an IRA, pension plan, thrift plan, 401(k), or 403(b) that will be available at retirement? What are your options with these plans? Can they be rolled over to your own IRA, or are you locked in to receiving a monthly income? Is there the possibility of an inheritance? Will the inheritance be liquid or a non-liquid asset that may have to be sold (e.g., business, building, residence)? Being put in that position can be troublesome. Have you ever sold a business before? It can be quite involved.

In summary, we must make a very good attempt to determine the value and liquidity of your assets. Defining these positions will help us close in on the bottom line.

Habit Three:
Know Your Income Requirements

We have to work backward after we learn your monthly income requirements. These requirements are determined by completing two budgets:

1) Before Retirement

2) After Retirement

Example: You are deciding that you want to have $10,000 of monthly income when you and your spouse retire in eight years. You have always earned the maximum to qualify for the maximum social security benefit when you retire at age 66. For this example, I will use $1,800 per month and your spouse will receive 50 percent of what you get or about $900 per month. So you will have a fixed source of income of $2,700 per month. This will increase as cost of living adjustments are granted.

However, you want $10,000 and you have $2,700 of fixed income, which leaves you $7,300 short. Where will you get the additional income required? You may have a 401(k) plan or a pension, or both, at work. If that is the case, we review these plans to see that you are contributing the maximum allowed. If you do not have a plan at work, you may have an IRA and you may have other personal assets that you have been planning to use for retirement. In many cases, your 401(k), pension plan, IRA, and personal savings could provide an additional $4,000 per month. That brings the shortage down to $3,300 per month. That's our target. That's the number one item we need to know. We have to provide an additional $3,300 per month and do it in eight years. This will also determine the type of investment we must use and how much risk you will have to accept. That brings us to the next habit.

Habit Four:
Determine Your Risk Tolerance Level

What is your risk tolerance level? Remember, risk is one of those dirty four-letter words that we must deal with. The others are loss, fear, and pain. You may not know what your risk tolerance level is because it is usually your feelings or an emotion that decides your tolerance for accepting market fluctuations. It could also reflect your investment experience. Did you lose money in the 1987 market crash? How about the bear market of 2000, 2001, 2002? That's why we recommend a risk tolerance questionnaire. It has 10 questions regarding your ability to sustain your position in light of volatile market conditions. "If you can't stand the heat, get out of the kitchen!" This little phrase sums it up pretty well.

If you have sleepless nights worrying about your investments, you need to reduce your risk. We call this the "sleep factor." It's okay to reduce your risk to provide a comfortable sleep factor if you don't have a lot of ground to make up. In our example, we have to make up $3,300 per month. That may mean that you will have to accept more aggressive risk to help you reach your goal or you may have to settle for less, let's say approximately $8,000 per month, if you are not willing to accept more risk. Your risk factor is something that must be determined and your investment strategy must be appropriate. You may change your risk tolerance levels from year to year as your personal situation changes. You should always review your risk tolerance when you review your results. Your risk tolerance level is the most important factor your financial planner needs to know before helping you select your asset allocation.

Habit Five:
Know Your Investment Spectrum

The investment spectrum is like a big super market where you can walk down the aisles and pick one of these and one of those to fill your investment basket. Over the years, we have seen incredible baskets of investments. Stocks inherited from your parents can be as many as 40 to 50 years old. Some of the companies no longer exist and the stock is worthless, but some of the stocks have been bought out or merged several times over and may have split. That stock could be worth 10 times the original price.

There have been oil wells, shale pits, silver and gold coins, and shoe boxes full of bonds. Do you have rare coins and no idea what they are worth? Do you own property in the swamps of Florida or the mountains in Montana? Certificates of deposit (CDs), passbook savings accounts, old 25-gallon jars full of silver coins, cash hidden in the soup can in the pantry? It's amazing to see how many different ways individuals safeguard their assets. The problem is that there is no consistency for a growth strategy. Some individuals have no diversification or have not positioned their assets to overcome both taxes and inflation. For example, you should provide a 2 percent to 3 percent increase in your income annually to offset inflation. Products and services are not getting cheaper. Medical and dental inflation is double normal consumer price index (CPI) inflation.

It has been our experience that approximately 7 out of 10 retirees need the same or more income as they needed while they were working for at least the first two to three years after retirement. Travel plans are expensive. The average dollar doesn't go as far as it did several years ago. You'll need twice as much to travel to Europe. Home relocations are more expensive. Downsizing may be more costly than you expected. You may have to accept more risk if you are committed to your goal, and that brings us to the next habit.

Habit Six:
Seek Professional Advice

So, when it comes to selecting your investments and choosing an asset allocation and rebalancing your portfolio annually, we strongly urge you to seek professional help. This is the part of your financial plan that can make or break your retirement goals.

There are some individuals who hate to ask for directions. These individuals wander around helpless and lost until they finally give up and ask for help. That could be expensive. They may feel that it is a sign of weakness to ask for help. However, in this day and age, having your own financial planner can actually be a status symbol, but we have seen clients who have persisted in doing their own income tax returns for many years, and we can see the mistakes they make. According to the Internal Revenue Service (IRS), millions of do-it-yourself taxpayers pay more income tax every year than they really need to, mostly because they prepare their taxes themselves. This can be very time consuming and a costly mistake.[4]

How often have you seen neighbors try to sell their own home? It is not a good idea. There is so much involved today that both the seller and the buyer are looking for unforeseen pitfalls down the road with this transaction.

We frequently see individuals who have been attempting to do their own investing. They point to the newspaper or financial magazines as their source of information and sometimes it works, but you wouldn't try to fix your own teeth, would you? No, you would get professional help. You wouldn't try to operate on your own appendix, would you? No, you would seek professional help. So when it comes to your financial future, why do you try to do this all by yourself? You should find an accredited professional you feel you can trust and respect to help you.

The professional will help you select the right type of investment for your risk tolerance level. The professional will help you select the proper asset allocation for your time horizon and risk tolerance. The professional will help you allocate your 401(k) or 403(b) plan assets.

The professional will help you select the highly rated funds with low expense ratios and historical earnings that will help you accomplish your goals.

You've heard that you can talk to some people until you are "blue in the face," and they still won't listen. Well, that reminds me of the bricklayer who decided that he could do the job all by himself. This letter is to the claims department of a health care insurance company. It amplifies the problem of one individual trying to do the job all himself.

Dear Sir:

I am writing in response to your request for additional information. In Block No. 3 of the accident reporting form I put, "Trying to do the job alone," as the cause of my accident. You said in your letter that I should explain more fully, and I trust the following details will be sufficient.

I am a bricklayer by trade. On the day of the accident, I was working alone on the roof of a new six-story building. When I completed my work, I discovered I had about 500 pounds of brick left over. Rather than carry the bricks down by hand, I decided to lower them in a barrel by using a pulley, which fortunately was attached to the side of the building at the sixth floor.

Securing the rope at ground level, I went up to the roof, swung the barrel out, and loaded the bricks into it. Then I went back to the ground level and untied the rope, holding it tightly to ensure a slow descent of the 500 pounds of brick. You will note in Block No. 11 of the accident report form that I weight 135 pounds.

Due to my surprise at being jerked off the ground so suddenly, I lost my presence of mind and held on to the rope. Needless to say, I proceeded at a rather rapid rate up the side of the building.

In the vicinity of the third floor, I met the barrel coming down. This explains the fractured skull and broken collarbone.

Slowed only slightly, I continued my ascent, not stopping until the fingers of my right hand were two knuckles deep into the pulley. Fortunately, by this time, I had regained my presence of mind and was able to hold tightly to the rope…. in spite of my pain.

At approximately the same time, however, the barrel of bricks hit the ground and the bottom fell out of the barrel. Devoid of the weight of the bricks, the barrel now weighed approximately 50 pounds. I refer you again to my weight in Block No. 11. As you might imagine, I began a rapid descent down the side of the building. In the vicinity of the third floor I met the barrel coming up. This accounts for the two fractured ankles and the lacerations of my legs and lower body.

The encounter with the barrel slowed me enough to lessen my injuries when I fell onto the pile of bricks and, fortunately, only cracked three vertebras. The impact of falling jarred the rope from my hand and as I lay there on the bricks—in pain, unable to move, the empty barrel six stories above me, started its descent and scored a direct hit.

Needlessly to say, I will never again try to do the job all by myself.

Author Unknown

Let the professionals do it. They have taken years to learn their trade and spent thousands of dollars for education, licensing, and compliance, and they will represent your interest better in the long run.

So where do you find a professional? Besides the Yellow Pages, we believe you will find someone you can trust if you ask a successful senior person you know, respect, and admire. They may have been working with someone for years, and that someone may be the reason they are as successful.

Okay, so after you've selected a professional to work with and your portfolio is established; it is now time to maintain and manage your investments. That brings us to the last of the seven habits.

Habit Seven:
Review, Monitor, and Rebalance

Once you've selected a planner you feel you can trust, it can take three to six months or more to reposition assets, complete a rollover, and set up your portfolio as planned. You may want to dollar cost average your assets into your new strategy. Some people feel they have done the work and now they can sit back and relax. Sorry, that's not the case. It's like planning and planting a garden. After the seeds start to grow and pop out of the ground, you have to start to weed and water. If you put in plants, you have to be alert for cutter grub worms. They can destroy your crop. They must be found and eliminated daily. You get the idea? To have a successful productive garden, it takes planning, patience, perseverance, and continued maintenance throughout the growing season.

It's the same idea if you want to have a successful financial plan. A good plan can fall apart if you do not maintain your vigilance. The definition of financial planning is "ongoing process of your everyday money-making decisions." If your plan is in place and the accounts have been set up and the dollar cost averaging is complete, it is time to select your quarterly, semiannual, and annual review dates. We give our clients the choice of how often they want to meet and review their plan. With someone who is setting up a financial plan for the first time, it may be necessary to review on a quarterly basis for at least the first year.

Why do you need annual reviews? You need to check your progress, reaffirm your financial goals, and determine your risk tolerance levels. If everything in your life is the same as it was when you began your planning, then "steady as she goes." However, a year is a long time and many changes can take place.

Your planner also needs your feedback to determine if you should continue to follow the same course of action or change your strategy. A good planner will always check your asset allocation to be sure you're still on track. Some investments may perform better than others and adjustments and rebalancing may be required.

Sometimes, your asset allocation becomes unbalanced because of a style drift in the funds you own. The prospectus gives guidance as to what percentage of each style a fund manger can buy. However, sometimes there are so many good buys in growth stocks rather than value stocks that the percentage may become unbalanced.

Your planner needs to know if there have been any family changes, such as births, deaths, marriages, career changes, and retirement. When will you stop receiving a paycheck from your employer and start receiving a paycheck from your invested assets?

That's a big day in your life. If you have followed these Seven Habits of Highly Successful Seniors, have done the proper planning, and stayed disciplined and patient, you have a good chance of accomplishing your financial freedom.

Remember, you must go and get it because it won't come to you. You must plan to be financially successful. So, **do something now**! Take action! Get out a pen and paper and start today to develop your financial goals and objectives.

Chapter 15

Making Your Retirement Money Last

Contributing Author Jim Spires

Congratulations. You're ready to retire. No more nine to five. Plenty of time to do all the things you've always wanted to do. Time to roll over that 401(k) and start enjoying life. But how much enjoying can you really do? After all, that money has to last at least as long as you do. No problem, you did a financial plan five years ago, assumed a conservative 8 percent return on your investments, and you are only going to take out 7 percent per year. It will last forever. Don't be so sure. Before you retire, there are five very important factors that you need to consider.

While it might seem pretty basic, the first question you need to consider is, "How long will I live?" The answer to that is, of course, "Who knows?" Perhaps the better question is, "How long am I likely to live?" Well, when you did your financial plan, you assumed you would live to average life expectancy – somewhere around 85. The only problem with using average life expectancy is that it is an average. Mathematically speaking, right from the start, if you used an average age as a basis for planning, you have a 50 percent chance of living longer. That, of course, is wonderful news, unless your spending was based on your life expectancy and you run out of money at age 86. A far better idea is to base your income plan on probabilities rather than averages. For a healthy 65-year-old male, there is a 25 percent probability that he will live to age 92; for a female, there is a 25 percent chance she will live to 94. For a couple age 65, there is a 50 percent chance that one of them will live to 92 and a 25 percent chance that one of them will live to age 97.[2] The message is clear: Don't underestimate the amount of time you will live in retirement. You must plan on living longer than you expect.

The next issue to address is inflation. If you're old enough, you can probably remember President Gerald Ford and his Whip Inflation Now campaign. Did it work? If you think so, I have a bridge I'd like to sell to you. Admittedly, inflation today is not nearly as bad as it was in the 1970s, but it doesn't take much to upset your retirement applecart. Figure 1 illustrates what just a 3 percent annual rate of inflation can do to your expenses over a 25-year period. For someone retiring today with annual expenses of $72,058 (annual expenditure for individuals age 65 and over with income greater than $70,000)[3], even a 3 percent inflation rate will result in your expenses more than doubling, to more than $150,000, in 25 years. Whether you spend $50,000, $75,000, $100,000, or any other amount, a 3 percent inflation rate will cause your expenses to double in 25 years. Clearly, people who ignore inflation in their retirement plan do so at their own peril.

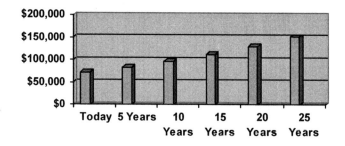

Figure 1

---

[2] Annuity 2000 Mortality Table; Society of Actuaries. Figures assume a person is in good health.

[3] U.S. Department of Labor, Bureau of Labor Statistics, Consumer Expenditures Report.

The next question on your retirement planning agenda should be, "How should my investments be allocated?" What percentage of my portfolio should be in stocks (or stock mutual funds), bonds (or bond funds), and cash? There are, of course, other classes of assets, such as real estate, fine art, jewelry, and lottery tickets, but for our purpose here, only stocks, bonds, and cash will be considered. A study conducted by Fidelity Investments using historical data provided by Ibbotson Associates suggests that longer planning time frames require more exposure to stocks or stock mutual funds. The study examined three hypothetical portfolios allocated as follows:

Portfolio	Stocks	Bonds	Short Term
Balanced	50%	40%	10%
Conservative	20%	50%	30%
100% Short Term	0%	0%	100%

At an annual inflation-adjusted (3 percent) withdrawal rate[4] of 5 percent, the study showed the historical likelihood was that the short-term portfolio had a 100 percent probability of running out of money at the 25-year mark, the conservative portfolio had a 60 percent chance of going to zero, while the balanced portfolio showed an 80 percent chance of delivering income after the 25-year period. While a portfolio that is too aggressive may cause a retiree to be overly vulnerable to market risk, too conservative a portfolio may result in a portfolio that fails to keep pace with inflation, which increases your risk of outliving your assets. The old saw, "Never put all

---

[4] This does not represent your rate of return, but rather the percentage of your assets that you withdraw from your portfolio for consumption each year.

your eggs in one basket," seems to be good advice when it relates to your retirement investments.

You may recall the scenario in which a retiree assumes an 8 percent return on his portfolio, withdraws only 7 percent per year, and assumes everything will be just fine. This is, unfortunately, not true. It is true that during your working/accumulation years, it makes no difference in which order you receive your returns, as long as at the end of the time frame, you have averaged your assumed rate of return (in this case 8 percent). However, when you start withdrawing funds from your retirement accounts, negative returns in the early years will have a significant effect on the portfolio's ability to generate sufficient income for the long term. To illustrate, assume a $100,000 portfolio earns 12 percent each year and the retiree takes out $12,000 each year. After 10 years, the account balance would still be $100,000. But what if the account averaged 12 percent, but had one bad year early on. Figure 2 illustrates this scenario. Starting with $100,000, the difference is startling.

Year	Rate of Return	Withdrawal	Balance
			$100,000
1	-10.5%	$12,000	$ 78,760
2	14.5%	$12,000	$ 76,440
3	14.5%	$12,000	$ 73,784
4	14.5%	$12,000	$ 70,742
5	14.5%	$12,000	$ 67,260
6	14.5%	$12,000	$ 63,273
7	14.5%	$12,000	$ 58,707
8	14.5%	$12,000	$ 53,480
9	14.5%	$12,000	$ 47,495
10	14.5%	$12,000	$ 40,641

Figure 2

In this example, the account averaged 12 percent per year, but the portfolio value has deteriorated significantly. And to add insult to injury, the withdrawal was not even increased for inflation.

All this leads us to the next question: "How much can I withdraw from my portfolio safely?" Another study by Fidelity Investments using historical performance data, again from Ibbottson Associates, showed that a couple with a balanced portfolio (as previously described), withdrawing an inflation adjusted 5 percent would likely exhaust their account by age 88. Considering that the probability of one of them living to 92 is 50 percent, it would seem that to exceed a 4 percent withdrawal rate would not be prudent. In fact, the same study showed that a 4 percent withdrawal rate would likely result in a portfolio that lasted beyond age 95.

The last question to consider is health care. While each case is different, and the costs can vary widely, a couple retiring at age 65 should expect to have medical expenses during their retirement of $160,000.[5] This figure is in addition to Medicare coverage and does not include long-term care.

By now, you have probably figured out that RIP (retirement income planning, not rest in peace) is an entirely different process than financial planning during your working years. After all, you cannot spend hypothetical illustrations, only cash. While there are no easy answers, the best place to start is with a realistic examination of your spending requirements. This list needs to be broken down into two sections: section one for necessary expenses and section two

---

[5] Fidelity Workplace Services; Sept. 2002 Health and Welfare Report.

for discretionary items. Couples should do this together, as what is essential for him may be completely discretionary for her. Essential expenses should be paid out of reliable sources of income, such as a pension (if you're lucky enough to have one), social security (cross your fingers), annuity payments, or withdrawals from reliable sources. Discretionary expenses can be paid out of other sources, such as mutual funds, real estate rental income, or even individual stocks.

One last thing, if you don't have a financial advisor, it would be a good idea to get one, as some of the investments you should consider are not simple. Even if they were, you should still have an advisor. You know what they say, "A lawyer who defends himself has a fool for a client." Remember, retirement is not like a video game, you can't just hit restart.

Chapter 16

The Missing Estate Plan

Contributing Author John Lau, CFP®, CPA, M.S. (Taxation)

Why the IRA Is a Missing Estate Plan

Outside of your home and investment real estate, your retirement accounts are likely to rank among the largest assets in your estate. You may already have estate planning documents such as a living trust or a will that spell out how your estate would be allocated and distributed among your heirs. But, your retirement accounts are different. First, the allocation and distribution of your retirement accounts do not follow your living trust or will.

Second, the tax consequences of retirement accounts are significantly different from regular assets. Third, retirement accounts are generally overlooked by estate planners and misunderstood by their owners. Tax-deferred retirement accounts such as individual retirement accounts (IRAs) and qualified plans require special attention and planning. Without it, as much as 70 percent or more of your retirement accounts may be lost to taxes. This chapter is intended to help you rescue your retirement accounts from unnecessary taxes.

For brevity's sake, "IRA" is used here as a general term to describe all retirement accounts, including traditional IRAs, SIMPLE IRAs, SEP IRAs, Roth IRAs, profit sharing plans, 401(k) plans, 403(b) accounts, and 457 deferred compensation plans, among others.

From a tax perspective, an IRA is income in respect of a decedent (IRD). Unlike regular savings and investments, it does not get a step-up in basis when you die, so it is taxable to your beneficiaries when withdrawals are made. Furthermore, an IRA is a part of your taxable estate, so it is subject to estate tax as well. With federal income tax rates as high as 35 percent, and estate tax rates currently between 41 percent and 45 percent, one can easily see how a substantial part of your IRA may be lost to taxes.

How IRAs Are Different

IRAs require special handling and attention because they are different from other investments and assets.

1.   Allocation and distribution

     Contrary to common belief, provisions in your will or living trust do not apply to your IRAs. Instead, what governs your IRAs is the beneficiary designation form. Make sure that you keep all beneficiary forms updated and stored in a safe place; and verify your information against the beneficiary designation information maintained by your IRA custodian. Do this, or your IRA may end up in the wrong hands.

2.   No capital gains tax treatment

     IRA withdrawals are taxed as ordinary income. There is no capital gains treatment. However, many people still think that because they have held a particular mutual fund or stock for more than a year in an IRA, it should be taxed as a long-term capital gain. This is not so. IRAs are funded by pre-tax earned income, so they are deferred compensation income. As compensation income, they are taxed as ordinary income upon withdrawal.

3.   Cannot be gifted

     Many people wonder whether an IRA (or a part of it) may be gifted during the owner's life so that what is given away would no longer be in the owner's taxable estate, and future distributions would be taxed to the recipient, presumably at a lower income tax rate. Nice thought, but no can do. While you may make a gift from your regular savings and investments without income tax consequences, this gifting does not apply to IRAs. The only way you may give IRA money away is to first take a distribution (and pay income tax on it), and then give away the after-tax money.

4.   Cannot be transferred to a trust

People frequently confuse transferring ownership of an IRA to a trust with naming a trust as an IRA beneficiary. They have very different tax consequences. For instance, transferring ownership to a trust would trigger immediate income taxation. This is true even if you merely register your IRA to your revocable living trust which, for tax purposes, has the same federal identification number as your personal social security number. On the other hand, naming a trust as an IRA beneficiary has no immediate income tax consequence.

5.   Distribution rules and IRA penalties

IRAs are subject to distribution rules. You should be aware of these rules because stiff penalties apply if they are not followed.

(i)   The 59½ Rule

With certain exceptions, you may withdraw from your IRA only after reaching age 59½, or Uncle Sam will penalize you 10 percent of the amount withdrawn. The Internal Revenue Service (IRS) calls this penalty an excise tax, and it is in addition to the regular tax payable on the withdrawal amount. So, assuming you are in the 28 percent tax bracket, you would essentially lose 38 percent of your withdrawal to federal income tax. As you can see, withdrawing money prematurely from your IRA could be quite a costly proposition.

AVOIDING THE 10 PERCENT EARLY WITHDRAWAL TAX PENALTY

Notwithstanding the general rule on pre-59½ IRA withdrawals, there are exceptions that may exempt you from the 10 percent penalty. While some of the exceptions apply equally to IRAs and qualified plans, others are unique only to IRAs or to qualified plans.

Exceptions that apply to IRAs and qualified plans:

1. Death (this one should be obvious, but it is a stated exception nonetheless).
2. Permanent disability.
3. IRS levy.
4. Withdrawals to pay medical expenses that would have been deductible if you itemize (although you don't have to itemize to qualify).
5. Withdrawals at or after attaining age 55 if you are terminating service from your employer. This exception applies only to qualified plans. It is not an exception for IRAs.

IRA ONLY exceptions

1. To pay for health insurance premiums during long-term unemployment (12 consecutive weeks).
2. For qualified education expenses.
3. For a qualified first-time home buyer ($10,000 life time limit).

SUBSTANTIALLY EQUAL PERIODIC PAYMENTS ("SEPP") – IRC §72(t)

In addition to the above exceptions, SEPP payments, otherwise known as 72(t) payments, are also exempted from pre-59½ withdrawals….with certain rules of their own:

The Five-Years/59 ½ Rule

Under the SEPP exception, the withdrawal amount must be computed using one of three methods generally accepted by the IRS – (i) the required minimum distribution method (RMD), (ii) the amortization method, or (iii) the annuitization method. Once the withdrawal computation is determined, withdrawals must continue for at least five years, or until the account owner reaches 59½, **whichever occurs later.** Severe penalties apply if the five-years/59½ rule is violated.

The No Modification Rule

After the five-years/59½ rule, there is the no-modification rule: Once a SEPP computation method is determined and chosen for computing the SEPP withdrawal amount, it may not be modified. An exception to this rule is that Revenue Ruling 2002-62 allows changing from either the amortization method or the annuitization method to the RMD method; but you may not change from the amortization method to the annuitization method, or vice versa; and neither may you change from the RMD method to either the amortization or annuitization method. Otherwise, stiff penalties would apply.

WHILE YOU MAY START SEPP WITHDRAWALS FROM AN IRA AT ANY TIME, THIS OPTION IS AVAILABLE IN A COMPANY QUALIFIED PLAN ONLY AFTER YOU SEPARATE FROM SERVICE.

(ii) <u>The 70½ mandatory distribution rule</u>

When you reach 70½, you must begin withdrawing from your IRA. A minimum withdrawal amount is required, commonly known as the required minimum distribution. Any deficiency (i.e., RMD not withdrawn) is subject to a 50 percent penalty. No, this is not a typo, and you have not misread it. The penalty for not withdrawing the RMD is indeed 50 percent.

Tax law mandates *when* IRA withdrawals must begin, as well as the minimum amount that must be withdrawn every year. The *when* factor involves two separate concepts: first required distribution year and required beginning date.

The *first required distribution year* is the year you turn 70½, and your first required IRA withdrawal begins with the year you turn 70½. Say your seventieth birthday is October 12 this year, then you turn 70½ in April of next year. So, next year will be your first required distribution year.

The *required beginning date* (RBD) is the IRS's way of letting you get used to the idea of having to start withdrawing from your IRA once you turn 70½. It applies to your first required distribution year only. Whereas required distributions must normally be withdrawn by no later than December 31 of each year, the IRS lets you have until April 1 of the year following the year you turn 70½ to take your first required distribution. The April 1 date is the required beginning date, after which all future distributions must be taken each and every calendar year by no later than December 31, or the 50 percent penalty applies.

Say your birthday is September 12, and you turn 70 this year (Year 1). Then you will turn 70½ in March of next year (Year 2), which will also be your required distribution year. But the RBD will be April 1 of the year after next (Year 3) because this would be April 1 of the year after you turn 70½.

> The RBD rule is different for IRAs and QRPs (qualified retirement plans). With an IRA, there is no exception to mandatory distributions starting at age 70½. With QRPs, the law allows you to defer withdrawals beyond 70½ if the plan documents allow it, and you are a less than 5 percent owner in the company that sponsors the plan. Deferral may continue until you actually retire from the job.

403(b) Exceptions

If you have a 403(b) account that includes pre-1987 contributions, the law allows you to wait until reaching age 75 to take RMD from this "old money." But any post-1986 "new money" is still subject to the rules summarized above (including the QRP exception). To take advantage of the age 75 exception, though, the old money must be separately identifiable, and any gains on the old money investment earnings are not part of this grandfathered provision.

(iii) Required Minimum Distributions

Once the *when* is determined, you must then decide the minimum amount the [tax] law requires you to withdraw from your IRA. The minimum withdrawal amount required is called the required minimum distribution, and it is computed every year by dividing the account's preceding year-end balance by a factor in the Uniform Life

Expectancy Table. See the RMD computation formula that follows:

RMD =   Preceding year-end IRA balance
          ─────────────────────────────────
          Uniform Life Expectancy Table factor for computational year

The Uniform Life Expectancy Table is duplicated in Exhibit I. This is the table used by most IRA participants in figuring RMD every year. But if your IRA's sole primary beneficiary is your spouse, and if he or she is younger than you by more than 10 years, then you may use the Joint Life Expectancy Table to find the factor in determining RMD. Using the joint life table would result in a smaller RMD amount.

(iv) Safe Zone: Between 59½ and 70½

In the safe zone between ages 59½ and 70½, the law is silent as to what you may do with your IRA. Whatever you choose to do in the safe zone, there would be no penalties or special tax consequences other than regular taxation on the withdrawal. This is where you may do some real planning with your IRA money—such as converting to a tax-free Roth IRA, Stretch IRA planning, and leveraging your IRA to a financial legacy free of income and estate taxes.

IRA Planning Strategy: Stretch IRA

The least that anyone should do to protect his or her individual retirement account (IRA) from unnecessary taxes is to take advantage of the stretch IRA strategy. Just to be clear, this is a strategy, not a product. You cannot ask your NEXT advisor to open a stretch IRA. It simply cannot be done. It is only a strategy to understand and implement. The idea is to enable your beneficiaries to take distributions over their single life expectancy. The objective is to keep the inheritance in an IRA to continue the benefits of tax deferral. Incidentally, an IRA beneficiary may not roll an inherited IRA over to his or her own IRA. The only exception is if the beneficiary is the decedent's surviving spouse, who is the only person in the world who has the rollover privilege. A non-spousal beneficiary may either take an immediate lump-sum distribution (and pay the tax on it) or keep the money in the decedent owner's IRA, and then stretch out the distributions.

A stretch IRA is sometimes described as a multi-generational IRA, an inherited IRA, or a similar name. The principal idea with a stretch IRA strategy is to maximize the income tax deferral advantage of an IRA. As a matter of tax law, the stretch IRA is pretty much automatic nowadays, unless the beneficiaries decide to take a lump-sum distribution. As a matter of practice, however, implementing a stretch IRA strategy is still pretty much misunderstood. Part of the confusion is because for many years, distributions of inherited IRAs were based on what is commonly known as the five-year rule. This means that an IRA beneficiary must either elect to take a lump-sum distribution or to stretch out the payments; otherwise, the entire IRA would be emptied out (i.e., distributed) by the fifth year after the IRA owner's death. Under today's tax law, this five-year rule still exists, except it has been modified to apply only when an IRA owner dies before reaching the required beginning date (April 1 of the year following the year the IRA owner reaches age 70½) and there are no beneficiaries named in the IRA. Even though the five-year rule has been modified, many people still think it works the way it once did, and they continue to advise beneficiaries of inherited IRAs based on the rules in effect prior to the modification.

S-T-R-E-T-C-H: A FINANCIAL WONDER OF THE WORLD

Stretching an IRA is one of the financial wonders in the world. The strategy is so simple and straight forward, and yet, it is one of the most under utilized and ignored 'secret' to wealth building.

The table below illustrates how a modest $100,000 IRA may be parlayed into more than $1.0Million simply by Stretching. You may have more than $100,000 of IRA, the tax-deferred compounding phenomenon is incredible.

Value of IRA when inherited

Age	Exp.	$ 100,000	$500,000
20	61.9	$5,881,640	$29,408,198
30	52.2	$2,756,394	$13,781,972
40	42.5	$1,329,456	$ 6,647,280
50	33.1	$ 678,471	$ 3,392,357

The above table illustrates how a $100,000 IRA account could, at the annual average rate of 10%, grow to a total of $1.3Million simply by stretching the IRA over the single life expectancy of a 40 year old beneficiary. The 40 year old beneficiary must begin taking minimum distributions from the account by no later than December 31 of the year after the IRA owner's death, but the balance not withdrawn stays in the

IRA and continues to grow income tax deferred. Distributions are subject to income tax.

The Mechanics of Stretching an IRA account

When an IRA owner dies, the beneficiaries named in the account must begin taking distributions. The first distribution must begin by no later than December 31 following the year of death. The minimum required distribution amount, under the stretch concept, is determined by dividing the beneficiary's single life expectancy in the first distribution year into the IRA's account balance as at December 31 of the preceding year. Okay, I know the verbiage sounds complex. Let's use an example as illustration:

Hank and Jennifer Example

Hank (father) has an IRA account naming his daughter Jennifer as the sole beneficiary. Hank dies in 2007 at 72, and Jennifer is 40 in the year of Hank's death. In stretching the inherited IRA account, Jennifer's first required distribution year is 2008 (by no later than December 31 of the year following Hank's death). The minimum required distribution to Jennifer in 2008 is determined as follows:

$$\frac{\text{IRA account balance on } 12/31/2007}{\text{Jennifer's single life expectancy in } 2008}$$

The IRA account balance on 12/31/2007 can be determined from the account statement. Jennifer's single life expectancy in 2008 is determined by looking up the IRS Single Life Expectancy for Jennifer's age that year. In this example, it would be 42.7 for Year 2008.

Subsequent years' distributions are computed the same way. The subsequent year's year end account balance would be used, and the single life expectancy would be reduced by one every year thereafter.

A frequently asked question about Stretch-IRA is whether one may subsequently un-stretch and withdraw more than the minimum required distribution? And the answer is yes. Stretching an IRA is simply a distribution option available to the beneficiary of an IRA account. The stretch distribution amount is simply the minimum distribution required by tax law. As long as the minimum distribution is met, the beneficiary may withdraw from the IRA account an amount over and above the minimum required amount. Of course, the more one withdraws from the IRA, the more income tax would result. Incidentally, failure to take this minimum required amount is subject to a 50% penalty tax.

In the Hank and Jennifer example, Jennifer is the only child and the only beneficiary in Hank's IRA account. What if there is more than one beneficiary. How does Stretch-IRA work then? Whose life expectancy is used? And does everyone have to stretch if only one desires to do so?

The tax law allows an IRA account to be split into different accounts after the owner dies. The responsibility is on your beneficiaries to ask the financial institution holding your IRA to split the account to as many beneficiaries named. By splitting the account, each beneficiary may take stretch distributions based on his or her own single life expectancy. If the account isn't split and remains as one, then the stretch minimum distribution amount would be computed based on the life expectancy of the oldest beneficiary. So a 10 year old beneficiary would have to take distributions the same as, say, a 60 year old beneficiary in the same account. And worse yet, if an entity beneficiary is named in the account (say, your favorite charity), then there would be no stretch whatsoever, and everyone would have to take a lump sum distribution since, for purposes of IRA beneficiaries, an entity has no life expectancy, so immediate lump sum distribution is required. This could be tax devastating.

Incidentally, an inherited IRA should be split as soon as possible after the owner's death, but no later than September 30 of the year after death. Get help from your financial advisor on this. Do not attempt to do this on your own.

What to do if you have named entity beneficiaries?

If you wish to name an entity as a beneficiary to your IRA, you should split your IRA during your life time. Isolate an IRA account specifically for the entity beneficiary. That would avoid any risk of forcing immediate lump sum distributions to your human beneficiaries, thus allowing them to stretch out their inherited IRAs.

Special rules for Spousal IRA beneficiary

If the surviving spouse is a named beneficiary in his/her spouse's IRA, then the surviving spouse would have one of two choices regarding the inherited IRA. One is to stay on as a beneficiary. The other choice is to exercise the right to rollover the inherited IRA to his/her own account. This second choice is known in the industry as a 'spousal rollover". As the name implies, only a surviving spouse beneficiary may rollover an inherited IRA account. No one else can roll over an inherited IRA. Not your parents. Not your children. Only your spouse, and only if s/he is named as a beneficiary in your IRA account.

What should the surviving spouse do? Rollover or continue as a beneficiary?

Rollover:

Rolling over an IRA inherited from a decedent spouse means the IRA now belongs to the survivor spouse, as if the survivor spouse has owned the IRA all along. This means the survivor spouse may name his or her own beneficiaries. It also means the survivor spouse is now subject to all the IRA ownership rules, including Required Minimum Distributions at age 70-1/2, as well as being subject to the 10% early withdrawal tax before 59-1/2. So if the surviving spouse is younger than 59-1/2 and needs to withdraw from the inherited IRA, then rolling over the inherited IRA may not be the right choice.

Continuing as a Beneficiary:

By staying on as a beneficiary of an inherited IRA, the surviving spouse may begin withdrawing from the account and avoid the 10% early withdrawal penalty tax (the 10% tax does not apply to distributions to beneficiaries of inherited IRAs). Incidentally, the surviving spouse may always exercise the spousal rollover privilege down the road (for example, after turning 59-1/2 when the 10% tax no longer applies). Unlike non-spousal IRA beneficiaries, a spousal IRA beneficiary may wait until December 31 of the year when the decedent spouse would have reached 70-1/2 to take required minimum distributions. For non-spousal IRA beneficiaries, distributions must begin by no later than December 31 of the year after the original IRA owner's death.

IRA Planning Strategy: Roth IRA

The Roth IRA has several advantages: While a regular individual retirement account (IRA) is income tax deferred (i.e., income taxation is triggered when funds are withdrawn), a Roth IRA is totally exempt from income taxation if the Roth IRA rules are met. So which would you rather have — income tax deferral or income tax exemption? If you have traditional

IRAs or company-qualified retirement plans, you may convert part or all of them to a Roth IRA. The conversion process is simple. You only need to get a Roth conversion form from your broker. Once the form is completed and processed, a Roth account would be in place.

Roth Advantages:

1. <u>No required minimum distribution (RMD).</u> Once converted to a Roth IRA, there is no required minimum distribution. Unlike a traditional IRA, you don't need to take minimum withdrawals when you reach age 70½. If you do, the withdrawals are income tax free. If you just leave the money in the account, any growth within the account is also income tax free. After your death, your beneficiaries must begin withdrawing from the account, and all distributions to your beneficiaries will continue to be income tax free.

2. <u>No income tax consequence, but beware of the five-year rule.</u> With the Roth IRA, a tax basis may exist within the account. For instance, if the Roth IRA was created through annual contributions, and because the contributions are not deductible on your income tax return, the account would in essence be funded with after-tax money. Therefore, the "tax basis" in the account equals the total actual contributions.

   Alternatively, you may establish a Roth IRA by converting from a traditional IRA; tax is paid in the year of conversion. In this case, the basis in the Roth IRA is the conversion value.

   Basis is important in understanding the income tax consequence of withdrawals from Roth IRAs. You should also be aware of the ordering rule, the five-year rule, and the 59½ rule.

Roth IRA Rules:

A. <u>The ordering rule</u>

In a nutshell, the Internal Revenue Service (IRS) uses a first-in, first-out method to determine the taxation of your Roth IRA withdrawals. Under this rule, the first moneys you withdraw are assumed to be coming out of your basis and, therefore, those moneys are not taxed (you would already have paid taxes on the basis money). Once the basis is fully recovered, excess withdrawals (over the basis amount) may or may not be taxable depending on whether you meet the five-year rule and the 59½ rule.

B. <u>The five-year rule and the 59½ rule</u>

To be completely income tax free, you must meet both the five-year rule and the 59½ rule. If you meet both requirements, withdrawals from your Roth account are known as "qualifying distributions." If only one of the two requirements is met, the withdrawals would be "non-qualifying distributions" and you would have to refer back to the ordering rule to determine the tax consequence. You may still be able to withdraw from a Roth IRA income tax free if you withdraw up to the Roth IRA basis.

So far, so good. It sounds simple enough, except with tax law, nothing is ever that simple. Here's the second layer of complication (or confusion, depending on how you view it):

C. Contributed Roth IRA vs. converted Roth IRA

Remember the basis discussion above? There is a subtle difference in the ordering rule between basis created by Roth contributions and basis created by converting from a traditional IRA to a Roth IRA. This distinction is especially relevant if you are under 59½ years of age.

If you convert from a traditional IRA to a Roth IRA before age 59½, and then withdraw from the Roth account before you reach age 59½, then the money you withdraw, even if it is basis money (and therefore income tax free), would be subject to the 10% early withdrawal penalty.

On the other hand, if you withdraw from the basis of a contributed Roth IRA, you would not be subject to the 10% penalty.

Why is this so?

If you think about it, the rule actually makes sense. Say you just have a traditional IRA and you withdraw from the account before reaching age 59½; unless you meet one or more of the exceptions to avoid the 10% penalty, you would have to pay the regular income tax as well as the 10% penalty on the early withdrawal. So, if you convert from a traditional IRA to a Roth IRA, you pay the income tax on the conversion amount and create basis in the account. A conversion before reaching age 59½ does not trigger the 10% early withdrawal penalty because it isn't a withdrawal. But, if you actually withdraw prior to age 59½, you would be liable for the 10% penalty.

What if you have both contributed money and converted money in the same Roth IRA? How would you decide from which "pot" the withdrawals come?

Good question. This is where the ordering rule gets even more refined. The tax law, in this case, again uses a first-in, first-out rule to treat the first moneys you withdraw as being from the basis of the contributed pot and then from the basis of the converted pot. Only when all the basis is recovered do you dip into earnings (or excess withdrawals) where the five-year and age 59½ rules become relevant.

D. Five-year rule clarified

The five-year rule begins on January 1 of the year when the first contribution is made to a Roth IRA (initial year), and it doesn't matter how many Roth IRAs you may subsequently establish, they would all be considered to start from the same initial year.

Example:

Assume Helen contributed $2,000 to her Roth IRA when the Roth first became available in 1998. She did not make another contribution until 2006, when she put $4,000 into a separate Roth account. The second account automatically meets the five-year rule because her initial contribution year is considered to start January 1, 1998, when she first made a contribution.

Roth Conversion

There are those who argue that you should convert only if you are young and plan to save the Roth money until retirement. This position assumes that by being young, you would live to see how the account grows income tax free and you yourself would benefit from the tax-free money while still alive (thereby making it worthwhile to pay the tax now for the conversion). I can never understand the logic of this argument. The fact is, once a traditional IRA is converted to a Roth, it enjoys income tax free status forever. When the owner of the Roth account passes on, his or her beneficiaries will continue to enjoy the account's growth income tax free, although minimum required distributions will begin after the account owner's death.

Conversion and Recharacterization

Anyone may convert from a traditional IRA to a Roth IRA if he or she meets the conversion rules, including the income rule and the marital status rule. These rules will continue to apply through 2009. Starting in 2010, there will be no more restrictions on Roth conversions – no income restriction, no marital status restriction. But for now, you may convert only if your modified adjusted gross income (MAGI) is no more than $100,000, and if you are married, you must file a joint return to qualify (unless you are separated from your spouse for a full year). What if you are single? You may convert if you also meet the income limitation test, which is also $100,000.

1. Modified adjusted gross income (MAGI) vs. adjusted gross income

    Adjusted gross income (AGI) is usually the number on the last line of page one of your Form 1040. Modified adjusted gross income, as the name implies, means it is the AGI after certain modifications. You will not find a line item in your tax return labeled "MAGI." It is a computation made outside a tax form or schedule. You should consult a competent tax professional to determine your income eligibility for a Roth conversion. You should be aware of two main items that do not get included in MAGI for purposes of determining income eligibility: (1) your conversion income and (2) your post-2004 required minimum distributions.

2. Tax consequence of Roth conversion

When you convert to a Roth IRA, the conversion is taxed as if you are taking a distribution from a traditional IRA (i.e., the amount of the conversion is treated as an ordinary income item). Incidentally, if you convert before reaching age 59½, the conversion income is exempted from the 10% early withdrawal penalty. But if you are thinking about converting from a traditional IRA and immediately taking a withdrawal to avoid the 10% penalty, think again. It won't work. If you convert before age 59½, and take distributions before reaching 59½, you would still have to cough up the 10% penalty to Uncle Sam.

3. Recharacterization

Congress has made it possible for you to change your mind after you convert to a Roth account. This essentially "undoes" the Roth IRA conversion and puts the account back to a traditional IRA. You don't need a reason for the recharacterization. No IRS consent is required for the recharacterization. But to make it effective, you must recharacterize in a timely fashion. You must "undo" (recharacterize) by no later than October 15 of the year following the original conversion.

Example:

Assume Adam converts a $100,000 traditional IRA to a Roth IRA in 2005. Adam files his 2005 income tax return before

April 15, 2006, and pays tax on the $100,000. In the summer of 2006, his Roth IRA loses about half of its value due to market volatility. Adam doesn't want to be sitting with a $50,000 account after paying tax on $100,000 income. Adam may file an amendment (by no later than October 15, 2006) to recharacterize the Roth conversion and get a refund on the tax he paid on the $100,000 conversion.

The recharacterization must include not only the original conversion amount, but also any income or loss attributable to the conversion amount. If your conversion was put in a separate account of its own, then the recharacterization would be as simple as transferring the entire Roth account back to a traditional IRA. But if the Roth conversion was commingled with, say, an already existing Roth, then the income/loss attributable to the conversion must be calculated using an IRS formula. If you run into this situation, consult a competent tax professional for assistance.

Leveraging Your IRA to a True Financial Legacy

Because an IRA can be taxed at both income and estate tax levels, you could lose a substantial part of your IRA to taxes. In addition to the Stretch IRA strategy and Roth conversion, another powerful planning option is to use life insurance to leverage your IRA to an income-tax-free and estate-tax-free financial legacy. The power of this strategy lies in the facts that life insurance death benefits are free from income tax and life insurance creates an immediate estate upon the insured's death (leveraging), which is not available with any other asset types. You may also transfer the life insurance death benefit out of your taxable estate with a life insurance trust (thus avoiding estate taxation).

LeRoy and Denise Example

LeRoy and Denise are married. LeRoy is 61 years old, and Denise is 58. LeRoy has $2 million in an IRA. Denise worked only a few years before marrying LeRoy, and her IRA is a much smaller $200,000. They have four children, ages 30 to 41. LeRoy is a nonsmoker and is in great health. He bought a $2 million life insurance policy naming his wife Denise as the beneficiary. He also named his four children as primary beneficiaries of his IRA. This is so that when LeRoy dies, his kids may inherit his IRA and stretch out distributions over their individual single life expectancy years, while the $2 million would also escape estate tax in its entirety because of the lifetime exemption currently available to LeRoy's estate. Meanwhile, LeRoy's spouse Denise will get a $2 million income-tax-free life insurance payoff to replace the IRA money designated to the kids. Her financial interest is protected, while LeRoy has achieved maximum tax advantage. Denise may then fund a life insurance trust with yet another policy naming her children as beneficiaries, thus further leveraging what she has. When she dies, her estate would pass on yet more estate- and income-tax-free assets to the heirs. This illustrates how an IRA portfolio may be leveraged to a real financial legacy.

How Much Life Insurance Should You Get?

How much life insurance to get depends partly on whether you have a taxable estate. The current law (EGTRRA[6]) provides for total estate tax repeal in 2010, followed by the lifetime exemption amount reverting back to the pre-EGTRRA level at $1 million per person. So, if you don't have an estate tax exposure now, you may have one after 2010. If you have a taxable estate, your heirs may need to withdraw from their

---

[6] The *Economic Growth & Tax Relief Reconciliation Act* signed into law on June 7, 2001.

inherited IRA to pay estate taxes. And upon withdrawal, there are immediate income tax consequences, which may lead to withdrawing more to pay the taxes…and then more income tax…and the vicious cycle begins. So if you have a taxable estate, you may want to at least get enough insurance to cover the projected estate tax liability. That way, your heirs would be able to keep the IRA inheritance intact in a tax-deferred account, while taking stretch distributions to maximize the tax deferral advantage.

An important goal in estate planning is to maximize what you can pass on to your heirs net of all taxes. Even if you don't have an estate tax issue, the leveraging strategy would still work, maybe even better, since there would be no estate tax to pay, and all the income-tax-free death benefits would go to your heirs. In addition, what is left of the IRA (assuming your heirs inherit that too) may still be stretched out over their life expectancy. This is IRA estate tax planning at its best.

Who Should Be Your IRA's Beneficiaries?

Beneficiary designation is an important IRA planning area for estate conservation. Its significance in planning is often underplayed. Most beneficiary designations involve naming the spouse as the primary beneficiary, and then non-spouses (children, nieces, nephews, brothers, sisters, etc.,) as secondary or contingent beneficiaries. Sometimes, IRAs have no designated beneficiaries or the owner has named his or her estate as the beneficiary. As one IRA owner said, "I have spelled out in my will how my estate is to be distributed. And since my IRA is part of the estate, why wouldn't it make sense to just name my estate as the IRA beneficiary?" There is nothing wrong in the logic of that thinking if you don't mind your heirs just ending up with pennies on a dollar from the IRA inheritance. This is what happens – when an estate is named as the IRA beneficiary, distributions commence immediately at death into the estate. IRA distribution is a taxable event, and all of the money would then be subject to immediate income taxation. And if you have a taxable estate, there would be estate tax on it as well. This is how you end up with pennies on a dollar left for your intended beneficiaries. If a beneficiary other than your estate is named, then at least the account's tax deferral status would be retained, and other planning strategies may also be applied.

Beneficiary designation is complex and may have significant effects on your taxes. You are strongly encouraged to seek professional guidance in this area.

The following individuals/entities are commonly named as IRA beneficiaries:

- Spouse
- Children/grandchildren
- Trust
- Charity
- Others – related or not
- IRS (usually by default if no careful planning is done)

Spousal Beneficiary

The spouse is by far the most common primary beneficiary named in IRAs. This is certainly the most logical, although it may not always be the most tax efficient.

A spousal beneficiary has more distribution choices when he or she inherits an IRA. For instance, a spousal beneficiary may roll over the inherited IRA into his or her own IRA and treat the account as if it had always been his or her own from the beginning. This rollover option is available only to a spousal beneficiary. Alternatively, a spousal beneficiary may, instead of rolling over the inherited IRA, keep the IRA in the decedent's name and stay on as a beneficiary on the account.

For example, Tom named his wife Clara as his IRA's beneficiary. Tom dies. If Clara decides to stay on as a spousal beneficiary in Tom's account (vis-à-vis spousal rollover), Tom's account would then be re-titled to something like "Tom (Deceased) IRA, FBO Clara as beneficiary."

There would be some real differences to Clara in whether she chooses to stay as a spousal beneficiary or to roll the account over to her own. An important difference would be in the 10 percent early withdrawal tax for pre-59½ distribution. If Clara rolls Tom's IRA over to her own, the account would be treated as if it had always been hers, and she would be subject to the IRA distribution rules as an owner. This means distributions prior to age 59½ are subject to the 10 percent early withdrawal penalty (unless certain exceptions apply). If Clara stays on as a beneficiary, the 10 percent early withdrawal penalty is waived. The 10 percent penalty on pre-59½ IRA withdrawals does not apply to IRA beneficiaries. So, if Clara is younger than 59½ and may need to rely on the IRA inheritance to live on, then choosing to stay as a spousal beneficiary on the account may be a better choice. Rolling over the account to her own name would expose her to the 10 percent penalty if she takes distributions before age 59½. Furthermore, as an IRA spousal beneficiary, Clara would have the option of either taking distributions immediately or waiting to take distributions by December 31 of the year when Tom (the original spousal owner) would have reached 70½. This waiting alternative is only available to a spousal beneficiary. For non-spousal beneficiaries, distributions must begin by no later than December 31 of the year after the account owner's death. Incidentally, a spousal beneficiary may always roll an inherited IRA over to his or her own IRA at a later date, if so desired.

Children/Grandchildren

With children and grandchildren, or anyone other than the IRA owner's spousal beneficiary, there is no rollover option. So a non-spousal beneficiary would either have to take a lump-sum distribution (immediate income taxation) or inherit the IRA as a beneficiary. If the inheritance IRA option is chosen, then the IRA stays tax deferred, and the beneficiary may take distributions over his or her single life expectancy.

Upon inheriting an IRA, the beneficiary should always remember to name his or her own beneficiary so the IRA stretch may continue through the remaining open years of his or her singe life expectancy.

Trust

Unless you absolutely want to control how your beneficiary takes distributions from your IRA, and you find no other way to accomplish this, naming a trust as a beneficiary does not accomplish much. Naming a trust as beneficiary would not give you any additional tax benefits. But if you wish to exert control on how IRA withdrawals are to be made to a beneficiary, then using a trust as your IRA beneficiary may make sense.

When a trust is named as an IRA beneficiary, the annual RMD amount (assuming the account is stretched) is computed based on the shortest life expectancy of all the trust beneficiaries. This is if the trust qualifies as a "see-through" trust.

Qualification requirements include:

- The trust must be a valid trust under state law.
- The trust must become irrevocable at the death of the IRA owner.

- Beneficiaries of the trust must be identifiable.

- A copy of the trust must be provided to the IRA custodian by no later than October 31 of the year after the IRA owner's death.

The Shortest Life Expectancy Rule

Unlike naming individuals directly as beneficiaries in your IRA, with a trust, the IRA may not be split after death to take advantage of the individual trust beneficiaries' own life expectancy for stretching distributions. Instead, the RMD amount is computed on the shortest life expectancy of all trust beneficiaries. This is called the "shortest life expectancy" rule.

For example, assume the trust has several beneficiaries, including a 10-year-old grandson, a 40-year-old son/daughter, and a 65-year-old grandmother. Unlike with individual IRA beneficiaries where the account may be split after death and each of the designated beneficiaries may stretch out distributions based on their own life expectancy, the stretch distribution amount with the trust in this case would be based on the life expectancy of the 65-year-old grandmother, thus losing much of the deferral benefits otherwise available to the younger individual beneficiaries. Worse yet, if a non-person is named as a trust beneficiary, under the shortest life expectancy rule, this would force immediate distribution for everyone else in the trust, losing all deferral opportunities. This is so since a non-person beneficiary has no life expectancy.

One way to plan around the shortest life expectancy rule is to set up different trusts for different beneficiaries. In the above example, if it is absolutely necessary for you to control the flow of IRA distributions to all three individuals, then you would create three IRA beneficiary trusts with a single individual beneficiary in each trust. That way, each IRA trust beneficiary would be treated on its own and each single individual's own life expectancy would be used to figure RMD.

Accumulation IRA Trust v. Conduit IRA Trust

Taxation at the IRA trust level depends on whether its provisions call for accumulating income inside the trust for future distributions or immediately passing on each year's RMD to the trust beneficiary.

If income is accumulated inside an IRA trust, income tax is paid by the trust. The trust tax rate is the highest in the land. For instance, in 2006, the trust income tax rate reaches 35 percent when trust income is $10,050. For individual taxpayers, the highest income tax rate at 35 percent is effective when taxable income exceeds $336,550. So, one must weigh the advantage of exerting control over IRA withdrawals against the potential higher taxation at the trust level.

With a conduit trust, all income passes through the trust and is distributed to the trust beneficiary. Income tax is also passed to the trust beneficiary. A conduit trust may be appropriate to mandate stretch distribution while avoiding the potentially higher taxes at the trust level.

Conclusion

IRAs and qualified plans are great retirement planning vehicles. They were put in place by Congress to encourage personal savings for retirement. Your retirement accounts can be your great friends (tax deferral), but they can also be your worst enemies if you don't carefully plan for their exit strategies. The Stretch IRA, Roth IRA, and leveraging strategies described in this chapter are to help you rescue your IRA from unnecessary taxes. Your next step should be to contact your personal financial advisor to design a personal IRA rescue plan for implementation.

Exhibit I

Uniform Distribution Table

This table is the new life expectancy table to be used by all IRA owners to calculate lifetime distributions (unless your beneficiary is your spouse who is more than 10 years younger than you). In that case, you would not use this table, you would use the actual joint life expectancy of you and your spouse based on the regular joint life expectancy table. The Uniform Distribution Table is never used by IRA beneficiaries to compute required distributions on their inherited IRAs.

Age of IRA Owner or Plan Participant	Life Expectancy (in years)
70	27.4
71	26.5
72	25.6
73	24.7
74	23.8
75	22.9
76	22.0
77	21.2
78	20.3
79	19.5
80	18.7
81	17.9
82	17.1
83	16.3
84	15.5

85	14.8
86	14.1
87	13.4
88	12.7
89	12.0
90	11.4
91	10.8
92	10.2
93	9.6
94	9.1
95	8.6
96	8.1
97	7.6
98	7.1
99	6.7
100	6.3
101	5.9
102	5.5
103	5.2
104	4.9
105	4.5
106	4.2
107	3.9
108	3.7
109	3.4
110	3.1
111	2.9
112	2.6